TABLE OF CONTENTS

The sermons in this book are not intended to replace your personal study of the Word of God! It is my prayer that the ideas and thoughts contained here will merely stimulate your own thinking as you study His Word.

Be that as it may, the sermons here for those who wish to use them for the glory of God. May they prove a blessing and help in your work as a preacher of the inerrant, infallible Word of the living God!

Sermon-Friends Take Friends to Jesus
Luke 5:17-20 and 24-26

<u>Introduction</u>: Few words in the English language hold as much significance as does the word friend. Throughout life, we seem destined to define people by the description "friend" and even go so far as to categorize them in groups [best] [good][friend]. The Bible says a lot about the word friend too.

■ In Exodus, it mentions that God talks with Moses so kind it's as a man talks with his friend.

■ In Job, after his sickness, he is advised to pray for his friend.

■ In Proverbs, it says that a man with a friend is rich in many ways.

- Solomon also says that a friend sticks closer than a brother.
- Further we find that if a man wants a friend, he must first show himself friendly.
- Luke tells about a friend that can be disturbed, even @ midnight.
- Jesus says that greater love has no man than this.."a man lay down his life for friends".

So, we believe today, that God had every intention to make friends important in the life of people. We just came by to offer you the joy and admiration of knowing that as friends we pledge to stick with you through thick and thin. Because friends are not known when things are good. The only way to really know if a man is your friend is to see if he comes around when things are going bad. See, a false friend is like your shadow. As long as there is sunshine, he sticks close by. But the minute you step out of the sun and the shade begins to cool your existence, he disappears. Bishop Woodard, Sr. and Supt. Anderson [real friends stick with you when you are sick].

If we want to see the portrait of close friends, lets look at these men in the text.

V-17 lists some important men [Pharisees][doctors of the law][from every town- not just a few].
But the verse says that *"the power of the Lord was present to heal them"*. They were also sick and didn't even know it. But I tell you..important men simply want conversation [talk; debate; filled with why; close connections with history; facts; figures; methodologies]. They do not want to know about God [goodness][grace] [mercies][power][love] just conversation [know anybody?].

V 18 tells us that some men [Mark identifies 4] brought in a bed with a man paralyzed through some act. It had altered his existing condition. Clear research showed he was not born that way. He had been victimized by a problem. Josephus [great Jewish historian] said he had been productive but that he had become a problem. He once owned a business but it failed due to his illness. Solomon said the rich have many friends. But the poor suffer alone. These 4 had not run out on him, so I classify them as real friends. The text tells us that they had been looking for a way to help this man. Carrying him is symbolic of advise to believers that we ought to "bear one another's burdens".

- Friends try every way possible to render help in time of need.
- Friends are not just good time buddies; they hang in through rough & tough times.
- Friends do not keep score, they love @ all times; and

pray for the best for others.

But we see here that friends take friends to Jesus. They were looking for a way to get him near to, next to, the master of life. They might have tried other things, but none of them worked. This mans problem had begun to spread. Paralysis [physical][emotional][mental][spiritual]. The fame of Jesus had begun to spread and the results show because there is a multitude that fills the house.

Vs-19 they reviewed every way to get him to Jesus. First they tried a natural way [tried to come in like everybody else] Man [drink][drugs][party][stay up & out][act ugly][talk back][no good]. But when they saw that did not work, they tried the un-natural. Salvation is unnatural [blood sacrifices][substitutions][living sacrifices, holy, acceptable, reasonable service]. Look at the obstacles [too many folk] we do strange things because of people. [saved-sophisticated][nice-nasty][King-crucify Him].

They recognized they needed to do something else for their friend. They took him upstairs. You can get help upstairs. Upstairs is symbolic of prayers.

- Sometimes you cannot get help downstairs.
- Sometimes people are in the way downstairs.
- Things hinder us downstairs.
- But take your problems upstairs.

They took him onto the roof. A tile roof signifying that this was the home of a wealthy man. Wealth is to be used for the Masters needs. [message to church]. But we must refuse to let any obstacle detract efforts to help our friends. Not only did they tear a hole in the roof; but also they let him down through the hole.

- Didn't they know people were watching? Didn't they care?
- Didn't they know people were talking? Whispering? Motioning?
- Everything came to a stop. This was for their friend.
- What would you do for your friend?

In Vs-20, we see a surprising discovery far different from other episodes of healing by Jesus. The difference in this case was not the faith of the paralytic, but the faith of his friends. It is important to have friends connected to the right sources. Jesus saw their faith. We have made it off the prayers of others. Here Jesus sees a prophecy that speaks to His own coming circumstances. Oh how He wished for faithful friends.

Paralytic [Man]	Friends [Jesus]
sick	sincere
counted out	counted on
diseased	determined
problem	provider

hurting	healing
burden	burden-bearer
debt	paid-the-debt
victim	victorious

Jesus forgave the man of his sins.

In vs-24, Jesus explained the reason for working the miracle.."so that we would know that He the son of man had power to forgive sins". He commanded the man to pick up his bed and go home.

In vs-25, the man immediately arose and walked out before them. They witnessed a dramatic change [message to church about the change in those that are saved].

- Picked up his cot [problems of the past] [disappointments that had him down] lay aside.
- Left praising God [not the aristocrat, diplomat] [not affiliated nor associated].

Jesus enjoyed seeing these faithful friends. He knew that in just a few short months, He would be faced with unfaithful friends.

- Concern about the greatest.
- Boasting about their love.
- Betrayed by a kiss from a so-called friend.
- Asleep in the garden.
- Denied Him when asked.
- Crisis @ Cross
- Unfaithful friends.

A friend is a person that walks in when the rest of the world walks out.
Oh, what a friend we have in Jesus....

- What man among you will not go after 1 lost sheep..then call his friends? Joy @ 1 sinner.
- What man would not prepare a banquet and send them into the way to bid his friends come.

Sermon – Now On Whom Dost Thou Trust?

Isaiah 35:1-5

<u>Introduction</u>: There are times in life when trust is a giant among midgets in question. Trust is the shadow of mediocrity that looms over the broad challenge of a special situation. It can be words of fright that come forth in the circumstances of fear and the unknown. Trust, who can find it when it is needed most? When issues and concerns overtake our sense of calmness and we get the urge to take matters in our own hands. Trust is so difficult to describe; so much so that it often clouds our skies of faith, ruins our picnic of a life, and troubles us to the point we choose to give up rather than fight on.

If you would look back over your lives, you would see that every now and then, trust ends up as ashes from the fire of burnout or the shambles of broken dreams. It is the end of a calamity that won over the wisdom that God brought us this far and would not desert us. Trust is comfort when we are standing in the line of good. But let problems come up to us and introduce itself to us and then trust runs away ad hides from our seeking and from our eyes. He may be there; but we just cannot see him [trust].

Adam/Eve [God-Satan]. Noah [ark-wine]. Abraham [faith-famine]. Jacob [faith-fooled]. David [eyesight-eternity]. Peter [ability-acknowledged]. Me [sometimes]. You [whom?].

- When illness is a garment you wear everyday?
- When you work all your life and seem to get farther behind?
- When you give your best and evildoers give their worst?
- When you are sad and everybody else seems happy?
- When those closest to you-betray you, deny you and leave you?
- When others seem to get their desires and yours are slipping away?
- When our church is struggling and others are growing?
- When we are broke and in need; honesty has gotten us nowhere?

So here we see a foreign king, one that would not know God if He appeared in the thunder, lightening, or flood, asking a question that all believers [non-believers] need to answer.."Now, on whom does thou trust"? King Hezekiah had come to the throne after his father Ahaz has reigned 16 yrs. Ahaz had been an evil king; so wicked that he plunged his nation into dismal failure to honor God. He led them into debauchery and idolatry by building groves of trees to worship rather than the living God. He issued decrees that denied entry into the Temple and warned citizens of the danger of being caught sacrificing or erecting an altar. He stopped choirs [singing], musicians [playing Zion songs]. He dared deacons [pray], musician [play], ushers [seat], altered Passover and tried to blot out the nations memory of a helping God. The record bears out that Hezekiah's father was all that a father should not be. For 16 years, Ahaz ruled w/o good because he ruled w/o God.

And if daddy was not bad enough, Hezekiah's son was worse. Manasseh, his son ruled for 55 years and makes his granddad look like a saint. His name means "one who forgets and although this man was young when he came to throne he speedily forgot all that he should have remembered and remembered all that he should have forgot. Hezekiah reversed all the evil his father had done and Manasseh reversed all the good Hezekiah had done. He brought religious apostasy, degenerated moral decency, cultivated a fanatical belief in idols, instituted a passion for false things, substituted rituals and asceticism for truth and reality, introduced human sacrifices, and promoted worship of the stars above worship for God. He was bad. He cut off anybody that opposed him, persecuted prophets, priests, and princes that mentioned it was not right to do what he was doing.

So here was Hezekiah, caught between 2 evil relatives; yet doing all to lift up the name of God. That lets me know and I want to share it with you that heredity and environment does not determine character. Hezekiah might not have been able to show his father what was right but he surely showed his son what was right.

And you would think that with his efforts to please God that he would have avoided trouble. But here is a record of trouble brought on a good man. Hezekiah had destroyed his fathers' idols, reopened the Temple, cut down his groves of trees, cleaned and sanctified the Temple; instituted worship again, restored Passover and all solemn sacrifices. Choirs [sing], deacons [pray], ushers [seat] musicians [play], and celebration reinstituted and the joy of the Lord was renewed and flowed again to the hearts of the nation to the pleasure of God. Hezekiah had practiced the words of a wise king [Solomon] a time to root out [plant] to pull down [build up] and set again a revival to reform the hearts of mankind to do the acceptable and perfect will of God.

But even after all this, after all this wonderful work on Gods' behalf, after 9 years of trying hard to please God, Hezekiah got sick. [Message for the Church today]. Story of his announcement, illness, prayer, and recovery. The church needs to note his condition [pride], his cause, his course, and his cure. After being granted 15 more years, one would believe Hezekiah had regained Gods' favor. Thus he could return to ruling, respond to requirements, and retire to resting on the promises of God. All seemed right with the world.

Sometimes it seems like that to those of us that believe. God is our all in all; our very present help in times of trouble; our leaning post; the joy of our salvation; the horn of plenty; a never ending source of provision; everything and more. The answer to every prayer; problem. But brothers and sisters, all of us have to be tested. Gold must be tried in the fire. Maybe we think we are ready, but God knows we are not ready. Moses; Peter; Elijah; you; and me. We think we are ready!! [**trust**]

Vs-1 tells us that after 14 years on the throne, trouble came. [14 years]. "Sennacherib, king of Assyria, came against the defensed cities of Judah and took them". Sennacherib is a symbol of something we had beaten in the past. Cancer [came back]; temper [came back]; memories [came back]; whatever [came back]. Defensed represents the thought of being prepared. Insured [sick]; account [debt]; friends [help]; job [income]; whatever [prepared]. We often trust in things we have beaten with things we have prepared.

Vs-2 tells us the enemy king sends his chief-of-staff to Hezekiah to list the predicament and intimidate him and the Jews to give up [medical results; no letter from child; investments fail; job hired another; promotion went elsewhere; church hired another preacher; relationship sour; boy-friend got another girl-friend; all can be a predicament. He wanted the news to devastate the nation and break their will to fight [pain-unbearable][time-miserable][conversation-betrayal] [co-worker-raise][terrible neighbor-car][no-good @ no-church [getting along][no tithe [blessed].

Vs-3 tells us that God never leaves us alone. In the midst of great trials and tribulations, God will either come Himself or send help through others. Elijah [brook-ravens-widow]; David [rocks-oil Nathan]; Moses [rod-staff-Spirit]. God gives Hezekiah some help. Eliakim [servant]; Hilkiah [steward]; Shebna [editor]; Joah [writer]; Asaph [bookkeeper]. Hezekiah sent these men to tell Sennacherib they would not surrender. In trying times, we need someone to lean on.

Vs-4 tells us the evil chief aide responds with disbelief. Do you not know the odds? All the cards are stacked against you. Where do you get this confidence? Cancer [beat others]; recovery [virtually unheard of]; prisoners [rarely released]; unemployed [brought down]; homeless, helpless and hopeless [eyesight [failing] hearing [gone] health [bad] money [broke]..Trust??

Vs-5 reminds Hezekiah that "I got your city surrounded". How are you going to get out of this? The chief aide had heard the words of the ambassadors and replied they were empty [crazy]. The chief trusted his power and an army he could see. [Message for the Church]. [$][job]; [health][friends][education][training][home][income] are not enough. Trust??

If I left you here, that would not be good news. The gospel is good news and needed news for the soul that thirsts for overcoming adversity. So on whom can we trust?

No-1, you can trust in God. He who has laid the foundation of the world on its axis and holds it in the palm of His hands is to be trusted. He who outlined the edges of the world with words that speak things into existence is to be trusted.

No-2, we can count on Jesus. He who went to Calvary to die for us is to be trusted. He who is gone away to build a place for us to come back and receive us to Himself can be trusted. We can depend on Him because he paid the debt of sin and redeemed us with His own precious blood. Would he now forsake us?

No-3, we can trust the Holy Spirit. He that has changed the nature of man and served man in the role of forgiveness and prepares man for a home eternal can be trusted.

Trust is a word that Isaiah considers greatly. Why? Because he had placed so much trust in Uzziah. But when Uzziah died, Isaiah could see God. But Hezekiah had destroyed false gods held dear by his father. And now his enemy wanted to know who was going to deliver him from danger, trouble, despair, …

- On mine arm shall they trust. 51:5
- Trust ye in the Lord forever; for in the Lord is everlasting strength 26:4
- Trust in the Lord with all thine heart…

The angel of the Lord promised to defend them; went into their camp and killed 185,000.

Sennacherib went back home defeated and 2 of his sons assassinated him.

Sermon – How The Church Can Grow & Prosper

Habakkuk Chapter-III verses 16-19

<u>Introduction:</u>
One thing in life that gets my greatest respect is for folk that can do anything from scratch. I am just amazed when people can simply whip us something that tastes like the best when they start from scratch. It is so easy to go out and buy the instant formula and add water or milk, stir, and feed. If the baby has never tasted Mama's milk, the formula is OK. It does not take as much to purchase ready-mix and pour it in a bowl, add liquid for stirring, pour in pan, and bake for an hour to get a good cake. Anybody that never had one grandmother beat and baked will never recognize the difference. In today's fast-paced world, we are quick to pop a frozen dinner into the microwave, wait for a few minutes and enjoy a meal after the reheating process. But when someone works all night to make food from scratch, I seem to enjoy it better. It is more work. It does take longer. But it gains respect because it is all the effort of scratch.

I believe God has more respect for those that do it from scratch. In Abraham's day, God could have allowed another to create children for the old man, and then used the adoption process to claim a son that would serve as Abraham's seed. In Noah's day, God could have let someone else build the ark and then permitted Noah to just buy it. In David's day, God could have let Saul conquer all enemies of Israel before David came to the throne. But in each case, God asked these men to do it all themselves from scratch. Nobody asked me, but just in case you are interested, why do I believe God respects folk that do it from scratch.

Well, one day He made a world from scratch. He spoke light into existence before anybody knew there was light. He used His own time and talent to let water run from beneath the earth and form brooks and streams and rivers and lakes and seas and oceans before a drop of water was even known. Then he made land to serve as boundaries so the water would know just how far it could go. He started from scratch. He even created fish and fowl, painted the sky blue, and clouded the horizon so the sun would not cook man before God was done. He made us in His image. So since he started from scratch, I believe He has respect for those of us that do it the way He did it; from scratch.

I can look around the room this afternoon and see how far you have come. But I cannot dream of the hardship and heartache you have experienced to get where you are today. If the truth were told, somebody said you couldn't do it. Folk in your home town probably said you would never make it. As a matter of fact, there are probably some in your own family, in your own church, probably some of them are here today, that said you were failures trusting in faith. And they were waiting to tell you that they told you so. But I came by to encourage you this evening. To tell you to hold on and hang in there because God is developing us--from scratch. And when God develops a ministry from scratch....there will be times along the way when you will scratch your head and wonder..."Where is the God that told me to do this"?

But when God develops a ministry from scratch, there will be times along the way when you will not only scratch--but also to scrape in order to survive. But I came by to give you some good news. You don't mind if I give you some good news do you? When those times come; and friendly faces turn to false faces; when pats on the back turn to stabs in the back; when up seems like down; and smiles turn to frowns, please remember that God is developing you from scratch. That is good news because *"He that begins a good work in you will be faithful to complete it"*. You may not have begun to scratch the surface. Blessings and benefits may be hidden just under the layer of trouble. *"But if we trust in God, with all of our might, and lean not to your own understanding, in all thy ways acknowledge Him and He will direct your paths"*

There will be those that come to join that will not want to leave their old ways before entering this new place. Some of those that travel with you will want more say once you have arrived. Many that stood back and waited to see if we would do it will be ready to jump on board just as soon as we get complete. Some of your strongest followers will find their resources and tithes shackled by unseen debt and burdened by loss. But I still know that God is a rewarder of those that diligently seek Him. So, be *strong in the Lord and the power of His might*. You can then see all the things that God can do, will do, and promised to do for those that have the faith to trust Him.

History:
Habakkuk is a strange book and starts off complaining. Although this writer is a prophet, he does not start off by gleaning the grace of God. At the beginning, he does not open by celebrating the substance and strength of our Savior. Bible scholars have suspected that the prophet is the son of the Shunamite woman that built a room for her pastor to respect God and ended up using the room as a nursery for her long sought-after son. Elijah granted it to her as answer to her prayer once he knew of her devotion to God. Although that same boy died, the woman ran after Elijah to Carmel, and Elijah came to the house, laid on that boy, and was miraculously brought back to life by Elijah in 2nd Kings, chapter-4. So it looks like to me he should have praised God for His help. At least thanked him for his healing. Instead of Habakkuk honing in on the holiness, happiness and healthiness that comes from the Holy Spirit, he starts off in Chapter-1 and verse-2 with.."*O Lord, how long shall I cry and thou will not hear"*.

You can sit there looking pious and sanctimonious if you choose to-but I don't know one single person that has not expressed that same sentiment. How long? In fact, this passage was written in the imperfect tense that simply means it is <u>not</u> a one-time condition. I don't care who you are – when everything seems to fall apart at the same time, that time can become a rough time in your life. How long? Recently, my pastor and father was struck with an illness that got the attention of my whole family; including the church. I admit to you that I have prayed for his recovery more times that I can remember. But one thing I admit in my patient belief is that I have asked the Lord of Life…how long. He has been my companion for all these years. My constant friend and confidant. And while my service has lifted a many burden, his sickness has me asking---how long?

Brothers and sisters if you read this text, you cannot help but notice some of what is happening to Habakkuk. One, there is crop failure. The fig tree is not producing and no fruit is on the vines. That means there will be no food, nor fruit, for the nation. No nutriments. No minerals. No vitamins. No strength for war. At the same time, there are no olives being harvested. No oil for the lamps. No anointing by the priests. The light in the tabernacle would go out and men could not get forgiveness for their sins. No grain growing in the field. No bread for the table. Sheep produced no lambs. No meat. No offerings for sacrifice. Calves were born dead and grown cows were dying in record numbers. Brothers, It was a rough time.

Maybe it has never happened to you. But somebody here knows about dreams that turn into nightmares. You bible-readers remember that one day a runner came to Job---and told him that his crops were on fire; and while he was yet talking, another runner came to tell him that his sheep had been stolen; and while he was yet talking, another runner came to tell him that all his cattle was gone; and while he was yet talking, another runner came to tell him that his camels were missing; and while he was yet talking, another runner came to tell him that his 7 sons and 3 daughters had died in a tornado down at the elder brother's house. When everything goes bad at the same time--- that can be a rough time. Even his closet companion, Mrs. Job, turned her back on God and offered Job some of the most terrible advice a woman has ever given a man.."cuss God and die". I tell you when every thing goes wrong, it can be a rough time.

Somebody ought to pray with me.

We can snicker and grin at Mrs. Job for her words. But tell me children, how would you deal with it?

- When prosperity turns to poverty.
- When happy times turn to hard times.
- When aspirations turn to adversity.
- When your blessings feel like burdens.

How would you deal with it? The only reason we get upset with one another is because we are not having enough trouble of our own. When you get your head under water, you ain't got time to watch anybody else swim. When you are drowning, you will not care about the style of another swimmer. [understand?]

Well, there are 2 things that trouble Habakkuk. Even today, in this life of plenty, the same 2 things trouble us. The first is <u>annual revenue</u> and the second is <u>adequate resources</u>. See, the figs, grapes, olives, and fields are symbolic of annual revenue. Annual because they bloom and blossom every year. But the cattle and sheep represent adequate resources because they provide a man with extra stuff to last beyond the year. This hindrance for Habakkuk and the hindrance for most houses of worship is poor annual revenue and inadequate resources. So if we are going to handle an old challenge in the new church, what must we do?

Listen, if you please. This passage has some helpful hints offered by Habakkuk that I believe will show us how to deal with old problems in our new place. If we allow him, this prophet of God will point us in the proper direction so we can handle the pressure of the new place. What must we do? Well, now that you have asked…

No-1, we need to <u>deal with defeated dialogue</u>. All through the first chapter, Habakkuk is hindered with his defeated dialogue. The first thing we do when things go wrong is we begin to speak with cold conversation.

- "I don't know why they decided to do it like that".
- "Girl, I can't tell you whose idea that was".
- " They must think money grows on trees".

In chapter-1 you find more criticizing than evangelizing. He offers more sour than power. More bitterness than blessedness. If the church is to address old attitudes and ideas as we begin a new space in a new place- - we have to stop defeated dialogue.

The Bible is filled with an optimistic vocabulary. *"No weapon formed against me shall prosper"* [optimistic]. *"Greater is He that is within me than he that is within the world"* [optimistic]. *"I can do all things through Christ that strengthens me"* [bright side]. A great philosopher said that when God lets us go through the fire—He keeps His hands on the thermostat so we don't get too hot; but He keeps His eyes on the clock so that we don't stay too long.

No-2, we need to <u>devise a direction of destiny</u>. Right there is chapter-2 we see God advising him to stop complaining and start considering. *"And the Lord answered me, and said, write the vision and make it plain upon tables, that he may run that readeth it"*. Don't clown, sit down, do not cry, dry your eye, grab a pen, and write my friend. Today, there is a lot of talk about vision. Seminars and conferences across the country are dealing with vision. Don't get me wrong, vision is important. *"Where there is no vision, the people perish"*. But we walk by faith not by sight. Your vision will never come into focus until you sit down and write down a direction for your destiny.

- A vision without action equals a daydream.
- Action without a vision equals a nightmare.

Our direction for destiny should include God showing us what to do—and how to do it- -and when to do it—or else we will fail. In our church, we need to set a goal to have;

- Excellence as the culture.
- Excitement as the classification.
- Expectations as the climate.

So, I'm just about through. I dare keep you too long. But if we are to grow and prosper, we not only have to deal with defeated dialogue; we not only have to design a direction for destiny, we also must be <u>dedicated to a divine doxology</u>. Habakkuk decided that if he was to grow and prosper he had to stop the pity party and begin to praise. Did you hear me? I said, if we are to prepare to take it up a little higher, we need to praise the Lord. When what we do benefits others, it will also help ourselves.

It is funny that Habakkuk does not praise God for what has happened instead he praises God in spite of what had happened. Nothing is growing, yet he praises God. Fields are on fire, yet he praises God. He is in the poor house, yet he praises God. The Bible says that *"when praises go up, blessings come down"*. So I know that a praising church is a prosperous church.

<u>Closing</u>: If you are to reach your full effect in the life of the church, you must learn how to praise the Lord. You can praise God anywhere anytime, and anyhow. In the wilderness like Hagar. In the streets like Jairus. In the fields like Isaac. In a lions den like Daniel. In a fiery furnace like the Hebrew boys. On your bed like Hezekiah. On the cross like Jesus. You can praise him anywhere.

You can praise him—anytime. In the morning like David. In the noon hour like Daniel. In the midnight hour like Paul and Silas. You ought to just praise the Lord.

You can praise him anyhow. If you are short like Zacceus. If you are meek like Moses. If you are strong like Sampson. If you are quiet like Hannah. If you troubled like Martha. If you are in a flood like Noah. If you are in danger like Nehemiah. If you are threatened like Jeremiah. You can still praise the Lord.

And, let me tell you what happens when you praise Him.

- Problems become protection
- Stumbling blocks become building blocks.
- Calamity turns to conquest.
- Complaints turn to confidence.
- Trembling becomes triumph.
- Ridicule turns to respect.
- Tribulation becomes jubilation.

- Sinners turn to saints.
- Death becomes a delight [I wish I had a friend here]

I wonder---is there any praise left in this house.

- Your money might be funny.
- Your change might be strange.
- Your blood pressure might be high.
- Your self-esteem might be low.
- Your friends might be few.
- And, your future might be bleak.

But you ought to make up in your mind..."that I will bless the Lord at all times"... and, "his praises will continually be in my mouth".

Can you praise him in difficulties?
Can you praise him in problems?
Can you praise him in tribulations?
Can you praise him...when doctors have given up on you?

Can you praise him...can you praise him...can you praise him?

He's been so good...He's been so good...He's been soooo good!

Sermon – What Is That To You?
St. John   Chapter-XXI   verses 18-22

<u>Introduction</u>: One of the great stresses in the church today is the concern believers have about others. It seems that large segments of church-goers over burden themselves with the success or sorrow of folk. It does not seem to matter what successes or failures we have encountered/endured; we simply do not want anybody to outdo us. We go so far as to pinpoint persons that are near to us [neighbors] and generally create a distrust/dislike for them based upon our belief that they got something/doing something/going somewhere we cannot. Somehow, they are thought of more highly/trusted more greatly/bowed to more frequently. It appears that others tend to show them more favoritism/yield to them more often/listen to them more intently. Looks like those we love tend to honor others instead. We choose to accept that those folk are just great @ home/church/job/school/community/life. And we worry about them. We must practice care not to set out to destroy them. For in God's time, He will separate the wheat from the chaff. So He gives us a question for thought today. What is that to you?

Here lies one of the great passages of scripture. Speaking to us about our attitudes held towards untold numbers of Christians. The Lord addresses an evil that if unchecked in the hearts of humanity will harm the work of the church. Today, we will see the idea within one of the strongest believers in the Bible. Peter, taken by his brother, Andrew, was one of the first men to be accepted by Jesus as a disciple. Peter had a real need to be seen/first but he worked in such a way that he did not want anybody else to be seen/first. Peter always had a motive to use and misuse others for his purpose. That is why God used him so well. So I feel strong in my spirit today, to warn our church [Christians everywhere] not to worry about how fast/fine/far others go/live/come. Please concern yourselves less about who got/gets/gives, God will ultimately pay us all [it's coming up again]. If I steal/cheat/lie/kill; at the same time I sing/clean/cut/teach, will you say "he is in everything" or "less for me to do"? If Christ makes your neighbor rich/poor; sick/well; w/child or without…what is that to you?

Let us look @ Peter and see ourselves. He came to Jesus with a hot temper. Volatile. He could disturb a dead man's sleep. His bewilderment was notable; his mistakes huge; his actions impulsive; his motives hidden; his self-assertiveness unpolished; his weaknesses unseen; his disloyalty masked; and all these were sheltered by a noble nature. [Us-today]. Peter was the only disciple that had his name changed [Simon-Peter (rock)]. He had so many special extensions by Christ; they are too many to list. But here are a few. Peter was the first to have God's grace divinely reveal who Jesus was [son of the living God]. It was Peter who was among the first to witness Christ's glory [transfiguration]. Peter, first Apostle to see the resurrected Lord [appearance]. Peter, first to preach the gospel after receiving the Holy Spirit [@ Pentecost]. Peter, first to be arrested and miraculously freed after his faithful testimony [1st persecuted and delivered]. Peter, first to receive Gentile believers [Cornelius]. Peter, first to be foretold about his suffering and death. But none of that matters to Peter, he wants to know what will happen to John [what is that to you?]

<u>The Frailties of Mankind</u>: Bible-readers will remember that after the Lord's resurrection, He questions Peter 3 times about his love for the Master. Having denied Him 3 times, Peter is brought face-to-face with Jesus on the shores on the Sea of Galilee. Jesus had told Peter that Satan wanted his soul. But that the master had prayed for him. Jesus knew Peter would deny and desert Him, but He told peter, when you are converted, strengthen your brothers. Now that Peter has come ashore, Jesus asks Peter if he loves Him more than the others [Peter said earlier]. But if you look at vss. 10-17, you will see Peter say nothing about his superiority over others. You will also see that Peter admits that Christ knew all [remembered cock crowing]. You will also see Jesus use agape for love and Peter use philo [differences between His love & ours]. Jesus asked Peter about his love for Christ because the Master knows that before we can love/help man, we must love God first. [Yea, Lord]. But Distinct Service often meets man's frailties. So the power of Jesus' prayer restored Peter to his Apostolic Office. Peter dared for distinction; sought for higher service; craved compliments; cried louder about his unworthiness, but ultimately revealed it was all a sham. [us-today] What is that to you?

<u>The Failures of Mankind</u>: Peter, no doubt, did not enjoy Jesus questioning him about his love. But the Master knew of Peter's self-will and natural take-matters-into-your-own-hands way of thinking. So He shares that recognition of the evil nature within Peter working to control him will be replaced when the Holy Spirit comes upon him @ Pentecost. "You do not willingly submit now, Peter, but you will hold your hands open for the nails that will signal your death". Peter died too; upon a cross in Rome. In the meantime, follow Me! Paul says in Philippians II, "be ye followers of me as I follow Christ". This great fisher of souls; feeder of lambs; shepherd of sheep; caregiver even to goats, died on a cross. [must Jesus bear His cross alone?] So Peter was elated by his presumption; prostrated by his denials; cleaned by his weeping; approved by his confession; and crowned by his suffering. But as our Lord addresses Peter, he makes another mistake common among us. He turns away from Jesus and begins to worry about somebody else. [vs-20] Instead of keeping his eyes on Jesus, he starts focusing on another [he should recall sinking in the sea]. The text says John was following [obeying Jesus] w/o offering a single suggestion. But the text indicates that John's mind goes back down memory lane, and he thought about other events that showed Peter's envy. Definite Selectivity often meets man's failures. At supper one day, Jesus spoke about a betrayer. Peter looked and saw John on Jesus' breast and motioned for him to ask the Master who [use John]. When Jesus hung on the cross, it was into John's hands that he entrusted His mother, Mary [Peter mad]. When the

news got out that Jesus had risen from the grave, it was John that outran Peter to the tomb [showed Peter up]. After resurrection on the shore, Peter did not recognize Jesus, but John did [Peter was bothered]. On occasions, Peter wanted to use John, but that's all over now. He lets his envy be known. Immediately, the reconditioned Peter resorts back to a critic, converted to condemn. What about John? Will he suffer like me? Will he have trouble/sadness/sorrow/ will he be hated/ hunted/hung like me? You see the difference between these 2 great men of God. The character of each peeks out now; nosy/nice; noisy/quiet; kingly-kindly; questions/believes; tantrums/trusts; lead/follows the leader; slow to duty/slow to destroy. This Peterine tendency is alive in the church today. Rather than quietly accepting his role, Peter's mouth tells you about his heart. He said earlier to Christ, "depart from me, I am sinful [sending away who he needed]. He spoke to soon "be that far from Thee"; "Thou shall never wash my feet", "Why can't I follow Thee now"? Let us build 3 tabernacles here", I have never eaten anything common or unclean".

<u>The Falsehoods of Mankind:</u> Jesus rebukes Peter with the words, "if I leave him here until my 2nd coming, what is that to you"? Since my resurrection, I have all power in Heaven & Earth, so I can do what I will. By the time of this writing [AD96], John knew that Peter had died [AD67] and that Paul had died [AD68]. But the fall of Jerusalem had taken place in AD70, so John thought that Jesus had returned. [false] The theocracy of Israel had given way to the establishment of a new kingdom [Jesus spoke of kingdom]. How frequently Jesus has spoken today. Voice-thunder; sigh in the wind; laughter-rainbow; wrath-storm; growth-sickness; warnings-sorrow; notices-grief; signs-earthquakes & wars. But here in these 2 men are the characters of man throughout all of the dispensation of Grace. [Mary/Martha] [Servant with talent] [virgin with oil in her lamp]. Simon was bidden to follow, occupy, stay busy, and leave the rest to Jesus. John had passed into the sanctuary of holy love, encouraged to rest and patiently wait in silence. Jesus loved him. Born in the same year as our Lord, [4-BC], John sees death approaching and weighs the words at this scene. There are some great gifts and terrible tragedies to experience when we follow Jesus. Arrest @ Gethsemane & Care for Mary] [soldier sticking Him in the side & Him walking on water] [being told about great secrets & having great mysteries hidden from view].

<u>Closing:</u> You know a lot of us got each of us wrong. Many are mature in years; but act like children in character. We look like we know where we are going; but in reality, we are lost like sheep with no shepherd. We are young @ heart, but sick in the mind. We have been called grand names among ourselves. Disciples/ children/servants and apostles/teachers/preachers as well as members/saints/ friends. The book of Acts introduces us a believers/brethren/Christians/soldiers of the cross. The Epistles call us priests and kings. But others see us differently. We see us differently too. Salves/drunks/thieves/liars/murderers/wayward/good for nothing. But thank God today, He sees us changed. Soon we will have wings/

golden slippers/bodies that get sick no more/no fears, no tears, no death, no dying. Let us remember this; failure brings questions by Christ [not man]. Failure brings a need for repentance to Christ [not man]. Failure brings a need for restoration from Christ [not man]. Story of the Devil trying to tempt a holy man.

Sermon – An Old Challenge in a New Church

Habakkuk Chapter-III verses 16-19

Introduction:

One thing in life that gets my greatest respect is for folk that can do anything from scratch. I am just amazed when people can simply whip us something that tastes like the best when they start from scratch. It is so easy to go out and buy the instant formula and add water or milk, stir, and feed. If the baby has never tasted Mama's milk, the formula is OK. It does not take as much to purchase ready-mix and pour it in a bowl, add liquid for stirring, pour in pan, and bake for an hour to get a good cake. Anybody that never had one grandmother beat and baked will never recognize the difference. In today's fast-paced world, we are quick to pop a frozen dinner into the microwave, wait for a few minutes and enjoy a meal after the reheating process. But when someone works all night to make food from scratch, I seem to enjoy it better. It is more work. It does take longer. But it gains respect because it is all the effort of scratch.

I believe God has more respect for those that do it from scratch. In Abraham's day, God could have allowed another to create children for the old man, and then used the adoption process to claim a son that would serve as Abraham's seed. In Noah's day, God could have let someone else build the ark and then permitted Noah to just buy it. In David's day, God could have let Saul conquer all enemies of Israel before David came to the throne. But in each case, God asked these men to do it all themselves from scratch. Nobody asked me, but just in case you are interested, why do I believe God respects folk that do it from scratch.

Well, one day He made a world from scratch. He spoke light into existence before anybody knew there was light. He used His own time and talent to let water run from beneath the earth and form brooks and streams and rivers and lakes and seas and oceans before a drop of water was even known. Then he made land to serve as boundaries so the water would know just how far it could go. He started from scratch. He even created fish and fowl, painted the sky blue, and clouded the horizon so the sun would not cook man before God was done. He made us in His image. So since he started from scratch, I believe He has respect for those of us that do it the way He did it; from scratch.

I can look across at the old facility and see how far you have come. But I cannot dream of the hardship and heartache you have experienced to get where you are today. If the truth were told, somebody said it couldn't be done. Folk in your own town probably said you would never make it. As a matter of fact, there are probably some in your own family, in your own church, probably some of them are here today, that said you were failures trusting in faith and they were waiting to tell you that they told you so. But I came by to encourage you this evening.

To tell you to hold on and hang in there because God is developing you--from scratch. And when God develops a ministry from scratch....there will be times along the way when you will scratch your head and wonder..."Where is the God that told me to do this"?

But when God develops a ministry from scratch, there will be times along the way when you will not only scratch--but also to scrape in order to survive. But I came by to give you some good news. You don't mind if I give you some good news do you? When those times come; and friendly faces turn to false faces; when pats on the back turn to stabs in the back; when up seems like down; and smiles turn to frowns, please remember that God is developing you from scratch. That is good news because *"He that begins a good work in you will be faithful to complete it"*. You may not have begun to scratch the surface. Blessings and benefits may be hidden just under the layer of trouble. *"But if we trust in God, with all of our might, and lean not to your own understanding, in all thy ways acknowledge Him and He will direct your paths"*

There will be those that will not want to leave their old ways at the old place. Some of those that travel with you will want more say now that you have arrived. Many that stood back and waited to see if you would do it will be ready to jump on board now that you have finished the facility. Some of your strongest followers will find their resources and tithes shackled by unseen debt and burdened by loss. But I still know that God is a rewarder of those that diligently seek Him. So, be *strong in the Lord and the power of His might*. You can then see all the things that God can do, will do, and promised to do for those that have the faith to trust Him.

History:
Habakkuk is a strange book and starts off complaining. Although this writer is a prophet, he does not start off by gleaning the grace of God. At the beginning, he does not open by celebrating the substance and strength of our Savior. Bible scholars have suspected that the prophet is the son of the Shunamite woman that built a room for her pastor to respect God and ended up using the room as a nursery for her long sought-after son. Elijah granted it to her as answer to her prayer once he knew of her devotion to God. Although that same boy died, the woman ran after Elijah to Carmel, and Elijah came to the house, laid on that boy, and was miraculously brought back to life by Elijah in 2nd Kings, chapter-4. So it looks like to me he should have praised God for His help. At least thanked him for his healing. Instead of Habakkuk honing in on the holiness, happiness and healthiness that comes from the Holy Spirit, he starts off in Chapter-1 and verse-2 with.."*O Lord, how long shall I cry and thou will not hear*".

You can sit there looking pious and sanctimonious if you choose to-but I don't know one single person that has not expressed that same sentiment. How long? In fact, this passage was written in the imperfect tense that simply means it is <u>not</u> a one-time condition. I don't care who you are – when everything seems to fall apart at the same time, that time can become a rough time in your life. How long? Recently, my wife of over 40 years was struck with an illness that got the attention of my whole family; including the church. I admit to you that I have prayed for her recovery more times that I can remember. But one thing I have asked the Lord of Life is…how long. She has been my companion for all these years and while my service has lifted a many burden, her sickness has me asking---how long?

Brothers and sisters if you read this text, you cannot help but notice some of what is happening to Habakkuk. One, there is crop failure. The fig tree is not producing and no fruit is on the vines. That means there will be no food, nor fruit, for the nation. No nutriments. No minerals. No vitamins. No strength for war. At the same time, there are no olives being harvested. No oil for the lamps. No anointing by the priests. The light in the tabernacle would go out and men could not get forgiveness for their sins. No grain growing in the field. No bread for the table. Sheep produced no lambs. No meat. No offerings for sacrifice. Calves were born dead and grown cows were dying in record numbers. Brothers, It was a rough time.

Maybe it has never happened to you. But somebody here knows about dreams that turn into nightmares. You bible-readers remember that one day a runner came to Job---and told him that his crops were on fire; and while he was yet talking, another runner came to tell him that his sheep had been stolen; and while he was yet talking, another runner came to tell him that all his cattle was gone; and while he was yet talking, another runner came to tell him that his camels were missing; and while he was yet talking, another runner came to tell him that his 7 sons and 3 daughters had died in a tornado down at the elder brother's house. When everything goes bad at the same time--- that can be a rough time. Even his closet companion, Mrs. Job, turned her back on God and offered Job some of the most terrible advice a woman has ever given a man..”cuss God and die”. I tell you when every thing goes wrong, it can be a rough time.

Somebody ought to pray with me.

We can snicker and grin at Mrs. Job for her words. But tell me children, how would you deal with it?

- **When prosperity turns to poverty.**
- **When happy times turn to hard times.**
- **When aspirations turn to adversity.**
- **When your blessings feel like burdens.**

How would you deal with it?

Well, there are 2 things that trouble Habakkuk. Even today, in this life of plenty, the same 2 things will trouble us. The first is annual revenue and the second is adequate resources. See, the figs, grapes, olives, and fields are symbolic of annual revenue. Annual because they bloom and blossom every year. But the cattle and sheep represent adequate resources because they provide a man with extra stuff to last beyond the year. This hindrance for Habakkuk and the hindrance for most houses of worship is poor annual revenue and inadequate resources. So if we are going to handle an old challenge in the new church, what must we do? Listen, if you please. This passage has some helpful hints offered by Habakkuk that I believe will show us how to deal with old problems in our new place. If we allow him, this prophet of God will point us in the proper direction so we can handle the pressure of the new place. What must we do? Well, now that you have asked…

No-1, we need <u>deal with defeated dialogue</u>. All through the first chapter, Habakkuk is hindered with his defeated dialogue. The first thing we do when things go wrong is we begin to speak with cold conversation.

- "I don't know why they decided to do it like that".
- "Girl, I can't tell you whose idea that was".
- " They must think money grows on trees".

In chapter-1 you find more criticizing than evangelizing. He offers more sour than power. More bitterness than blessedness. If the church is to address old attitudes and ideas as we begin a new space in a new place- - we have to stop defeated dialogue.

The Bible is filled with an optimistic vocabulary. *"No weapon formed against me shall prosper"* [optimistic]. *"Greater is He that is within me than he that is within the world"* [optimistic]. *"I can do all things through Christ that strengthens me"* [bright side]. A great philosopher said that when God lets us go through the fire—He keeps His hands on the thermostat so we don't get too hot; but He keeps His eyes on the clock so that we don't stay too long.

No-2, we need to <u>devise a direction of destiny</u>. Right there is chapter-2 we see God advising him to stop complaining and start considering. *"And the Lord answered me, and said, write the vision and make it plain upon tables, that he may run that readeth it"*. Don't clown, sit down, do not cry, dry your eye, grab a pen, and write my friend. Today, there is a lot of talk about vision. Seminars and conferences across the country are dealing with vision. Don't get me wrong, vision is important. *"Where there is no vision, the people perish"*. But we walk by faith not by sight. Your vision will never come into focus until you sit down and write down a direction for your destiny.

- A vision without action equals a daydream.
- Action without a vision equals a nightmare.

Our direction for destiny should include God showing us what to do—and how to do it- -and when to do it—or else we will fail. In our church

- Excellence is the culture.
- Exciting is the classification.

- Expecting is the climate.

So, I'm just about through. I dare keep you too long. But if we are to handle old challenges in the new church, we not only have to deal with defeated dialogue; we not only have to design a direction for destiny, we also must be <u>dedicated to a divine doxology</u>. Habakkuk decided that if he was to meet the old challenge he had to stop the pity party and begin to praise. Did you hear me? I said if we are to prepare to take it up a little higher, we need to praise the Lord.

It is funny that Habakkuk does not praise God for what has happened instead he praises God in spite of what had happened. Nothing is growing yet he praises God. Fields are on fire, yet he praises God. The Bible says that *"when praises go up, blessings come down"*. So I know that a praising church is a prosperous church.

<u>Closing</u>: If you are to reach your full effect in the life of the church, you must learn how to praise the Lord. You can praise God anywhere anytime, and anyhow. In the wilderness like Hagar. In the streets like Jairus. In the fields like Isaac. In a lions den like Daniel. In a fiery furnace like the Hebrew boys. On your bed like Hezekiah. On the cross like Jesus. You can praise him anywhere.

You can praise him—anytime. In the morning like David. In the noon hour like Daniel. In the midnight hour like Paul and Silas. You ought to just praise the Lord.

You can praise him anyhow. If you are short like Zacceus. If you are meek like Moses. If you are strong like Sampson. If you are quiet like Hannah. If you troubled like Martha. If you are in a flood like Noah. If you are in danger like Nehemiah. If you are threatened like Jeremiah. You can still praise the Lord.

And, let me tell you what happens when you praise Him.
- Problems become protection
- Stumbling blocks become building blocks.
- Calamity turns to conquest.
- Complaints turn to confidence.
- Trembling becomes triumph.
- Ridicule turns to respect.
- Tribulation becomes jubilation.
- Sinners turn to saints.
- Death becomes a delight [I wish I had a friend here]

I wonder---is there any praise left in this house.
- Your money might be funny.
- Your change might be strange.
- Your blood pressure might be high.

- Your self-esteem might be low.
- Your friends might be few.
- And, your future might be bleak.

But you ought to make up in your mind…"that I will bless the Lord at all times"… and, "his praises will continually be in my mouth".

Can you praise him in difficulties?
Can you praise him in problems?
Can you praise him in tribulations?
Can you praise him…when doctors have given up on you?

Can you praise him…can you praise him…can you praise him?

He's been so good…He's been so good…He's been soooo good!

Sermon-I Almost Let Go
Luke VIII: Verses 43-48

<u>Introduction</u>: Throughout life's history, there is the repeated story of men that almost gave up. It seems to be the acceptable pattern that marks the path from failure to success. Emotionally, financially [business], athletically, educationally, romantically, yes, even spiritually. As Christians we must remember that seldom do we see our Lord worried about the same things we worry about. Jobs [employer], residents [Legion-Lepers-Lost], travel [walked], friends, family, but he worried more about our relationship with the Father. But here in this passage, Christ wants us to see ourselves. Although the main character is a woman, she is the picture of society at its worst. But He lets us know what can happen if and when we learn to trust the best.

<u>Desperation</u>: She pictures all people apart from God. Her problem is revealed in 1 verse.

Physically Desperate [all health was gone] we are ever moving towards death.

Mentally Desperate [all thoughts were on getting well] our wayward focus.

Emotionally Desperate [unstable due to a poor future] angry, betrayed, mad, hot.

Financially Desperate [all money gone] we cannot buy the things we need.

Spiritually Desperate [could not enter the Church] our sin separates us from God.

Yes, she was desperate. But usually we seek Christ when we are desperate.

<u>Determination</u>: She had plenty obstacles to overcome. "She came from behind".

The crowd surrounding Him [society]

The attitude of His disciples [church]

The importance of His mission [on His way to heal another]

The appearance of the needy woman [pale; poor; pitiful]

Yes, there were obstacles for her just like us, but we need her determination.

<u>Deliverance</u>: Her deliverance came from her contact with the Great Physician.

The touch of faith [everything she had tried had failed]

The touch was personal [she said if I…not if someone else].

The touch was sensitive [Christ turned and asked.."Who touched me"?].

The touch was genuine [something has been taken from our Lord-virtue (authority)

Many that surrounded Jesus never touched Him.

<u>Declaration</u>: In every encounter, there is an outcome [equal and opposite reaction]

Her trembling [we ought to be afraid of the Perfect One] but come boldly.

Her testimony [was sick and healed immediately] knew her prognosis.

Her respect [she fell down before Him] gave Him honor before all the people.

Her recognition [He called her daughter] Jesus assured her of how she was healed.

He overcame her superstition. Faith not medicine had made her well.

<u>Conclusion</u>: This woman represents us because we all have sinned and come short.

Time [important to see that time was mentioned and played a part] 12 years.

Condition [important because she had dismissed what stood in the way].

- Health (sometimes its our family)
- Wealth (sometimes its our finances)

Situation [as we are] [just one among the crowd]

Reward [we often get more than requested] healed and adopted.

There have been many that almost let go. [David-Elijah-Jeremiah] pretty good company.

Jesus almost let go. But he prayed.

Sermon – Preserved For A Promise

Hebrews VI: 9-12 & Joshua XIV: 6-12

<u>Introduction</u>: When a child, I saw the making of preserves. I saw the process that required food [fruit] and jars and rings and a top to seal. The thing that I remembered most was that the good stuff was on the inside. Nasty beets could have sugar added to them and sealed so that when eaten later those that ate would compliment how sweet the beets were. [Holy Spirit].

The word preserves means to observe beforehand. But it also means to keep from harm, danger, spoil, and rot for a future use. The word promises means a pledge to do [or not to do] something. In my youth a promise meant that a man's word was his bond [reputation]

So the writer of Hebrews uses the written record of Scriptural history to prove or justify his waiting and working until the saved becomes willing. It seemed so long in coming that the writer often had to remind himself of the patience Christ had exhibited as He came to seek and to save those that were lost. We tire so soon [examples]. We get defeated so quickly [examples]. We jump to conclusions so fast [examples]. But the Apostle that wrote this book wanted to remind us that we have to trust Him and never doubt; surely He will bring us out.

<u>Patience pays Off</u>: In verse 9, the writer simply says that patience will pay off. He seems to be hoping for better things. Caleb is the example presented this morning of someone that starts off unknown and almost unworthy. Born as a slave in Egypt, we know nothing about him until he is chosen by Moses to represent the tribe of Judah as the age of 40. We know nothing about him but that does not mean that God knew nothing about him. You do not have to make history to make the team. Caleb meant something to God and God used this unlikely man in a strange situation to show his faith. Caleb was to be a spiritual spy. The children of Israel have come to the land of Canaan for the 1st time and are to go in and take it. But they have seen giants [obstacles] that strike fear in their hearts. So they plan to check the land out and hear what the spies have to say. [listening to man rather than God]. The Bible says that Caleb knew that Abraham, Sarah, Isaac, and Jacob had been buried near the hill of Hebron in a cave. So he went there to see how their gravesites were doing. Yes, he spotted the giants but he trusted the Father more than he feared the folk. He reported, "we can take the land". Not for Moses. Not to keep people quiet. Not just to go against others. But for full conviction of the truth. He followed completely the Lord. That is what supports our actions. Our faith. Faith without works is dead. So look around and see evidences of our faith. Is our church growing? Is our church together? Are we looking for challenges due to my preaching or are you really trusting in your own instincts to discover that you think we ought to do?

<u>Providence Remembers Promises</u>. In verse 10, the writer reminds us that

providence [God] always remembers a promise. Men sometimes forget [debts, friendships, relationships, spouses]. Conditions change but not God [broke, jobs, sickness]. God will not forget your contributions. After returning from spying out the land, Caleb and Joshua were the only ones that felt they could overtake the cities. The other 10 spies agreed that Canaan had plenty of good food. They said the land had grapes like never seen before and flowed with delicacies just as God had described. [How did God know that yet not know they could take the land?] But they mentioned that God seemed to leave out the part about the giants. Do you see selective points-of-view? God was right about where the land was. God was right about what the land held. But God is wrong about our abilities to conquer it. [Does that sound like us?]. God listened to their defeatist attitudes and sent them wandering another 38 years in the desert. A short time later, a plague came upon the camp and killed 14,700 men, as well as the 10 lying spies. But God goes even further to recall what we do for the saints. Paul said.."be not weary in well doing, for in due season you shall reap a harvest of blessings". So God promises Caleb through the voice of Moses that he will receive the mount of Hebron. The words.."everywhere your foot troddeth shall be yours" are words that ought to give the true believer comfort. So when the children of Israel came back to Canaan, Caleb went up to ask for his portion.

<u>Perseverance Will Be Justified</u>: In verse 11, the book tells us that if we hold out, our wait will prove fruitful. Caleb tells us that he was kept alive by God. The trek through the desert brought great discomforts. There were common perils like exhaustion. There were special perils like the plague mentioned earlier. There were problems with sicknesses and losses associated with war. There were days of bitterness and water that was not sweet. There were cheaters and gamblers and thieves [Achan] and unbelievers along the trip [manna, gold, grumblers, murmurers, etc.] He was surrounded by the same kind of folk we see here in our nation. But he was diligent in his service. Faithful in spite of the faults. Yes, there were those that tried to sway him from God, yet he held on to his faith. And that faith paid off. The writer of Hebrews is holding out the same hope for us today. At the age of 85, they come into the land and begin to divide it. The 45 years added to Caleb's life is 38 years of walking with the wounded and unfaithful; praying that his faith will affect them more than their doubt will affect him. And 7 years of wars as they finally take Canaan. So here they are, finally, home at last. And Caleb reminds Joshua of what God promised him 45 years earlier. How long have you waited for dreams to come true?

You know, the longer we live, the more aware we ought to become of God's goodness. Caleb recognized that God kept him alive for some reason. We would do well to seek and discover why God has left us here so long. [Friends gone][Loved ones gone][Sicknesses][hurt and pain] [disappointments][sins][Surgeries][backsliding][jail][fornications]. But we ought to know more about Him.

We ought to know that God always gives more than He promises. [Solomon] [Simeon and Anna].

<u>Practice Makes Perfect</u>: In verse 12, the writer encourages us to stop being lazy. We make excuses about everything. We do what we want to do but find a reason not to do what we don't want to do. We have pity parties. Cry over spilled milk. Just look for ways to block our blessings. Practice makes perfect. Whatever we practice, that is what we get right. Caleb not only reminded Joshua of God's promise, he went on to tell Joshua that his mental edge was still solid. He knew there were yet giants [Anak] in Hebron. Your problems are going to remain until you use faith to destroy them. These giants had also been allowed by God to stay there for 45 years. After Caleb told of God's goodness, he told of God's might and power. Caleb knew he would defeat Anak because God had promised him. "Be of good courage and not afraid for I have overcome the world". As true believer, we must exercise faith [believe in the unseen as though it exists] and patience [wait, wait I say upon the Lord] and we shall inherit the things He has stored up for us, even in old age.

Closing: God knew Caleb's heart. After getting the victory over the giants, there was another battle Caleb had to fight. Hebron was to be a place for the priests [tithes] and a place for the city of refuge [help for the sinner] and he had to willingly yield it to Joshua. That lets me know and I stopped by today to tell you..that God needs things he gives to you. And the reason we get so few things, the reason what we have stops working so quick, the reason stuff fails and is hard to replace is that we did not do what we were supposed to do with them in the first place.

Sermon - Life's Greatest Question
Acts XVI verses 26-31

<u>Introduction</u>: Questions form life's basic aim @ the bullseye of intellect and growth. Most of what we accomplish, who we are, & hope to achieve has been spotted at the starting line of questions. Will you marry me? Did I get the job? How much does it pay? Is it a boy or a girl? Where does it hurt? Doc, what do I have? Will I get well? How long do I have to live? [not life's greatest?]
One of life's great questions is seen in America's courthouses every day. [guilty or innocent?]
But God and the Bible also ask some serious questions. Adam, where art thou? Eve, what is this that thou has done? How long halt ye between 2 opinions? Throughout the book they echo. Will you also go away? Are you also blind?

But here in this text, we have a man asking life's greatest question. "What must I do to be saved?
It comes out of the strangest set of circumstances. Preachers. Doing God's will. Arrested. Beaten. Jailed. Then, right in the midst of their trials, they rejoice, praise, and sing unto God [churchfolk].
God acts by dispatching an earthquake to Philippi to address His own [sends Jesus, furnace, dove, whirlwind, storm, clouds, lions den, sickness, loss of job, acts to children]. He shows up!

<u>False Sense of Security</u>:
- Security. [Paul and Silas were locked up]. He could sleep during this crisis. Weather was cool and calm. No earthquake was expected. We know not what awaits us. [Dad's sickness][children adjustments] [loss of jobs] But when we least expect it, God shows up. Earthquake is severe. V-26 [shakes foundation of jail][broke doors, hinges, locks][broke handcuffs of all prisoners]. But the impact of Paul and Silas denies them a desire for escape. [Christians impact the world (in it but not of it)].
- Position. [This man was the head jailer]. He could go home and sleep. He made enough to have a family and servants. His possessions were only one paycheck from dissolving.
- Respect. [The towns' people trusted him]. Into his hands men of trouble were placed. The Jews trusted him. All respected him.

Operates from Self Sufficiency:

- Educated. [built the prison on a solid foundation]. He used solitary confinement on his most dangerous prisoners. Employed the latest techniques in law enforcement.
- Protected. [carried his sword @ all times]
- Honorable. [took an oath to uphold the laws and constitution of Rome]. Held dear his responsibilities as Jailer. Would have killed himself due to failure to keep men jailed. He honored man's code more than he did God's code.
- Egotistical. [paranoia set in when he saw the condition of the jail with his eyes]. He was working out of ignorance because he had to call for a light [Jesus is the light of the world]. He never expected the men to remain even if they had the chance to escape.

Arrive at Point of Recognition:

- See the Differences. [When Paul called out that "we are all here", the jailer knew there were differences between him and these men]. Jesus was different. As Christians we too must be different. Instead of fussing and disagreeing, we need to offer a shoulder of trust and listen to His voice. "Come unto me all who are heavy laden, and I will give you rest".
- Forsake Other Refuges. [city of refuge]. This jailer was awakened from his slumber of sin. He comes with sincere inquiry [false believers]. His question is not mere curiosity. Simple speculation like ours [clothes, jewelry, cars, hats, shout, sing, preach]. He had a hungry soul that awaited brotherly sympathy. [recognizing the saved by how we treat each other]
- Appealed to Truth. [only truth could hold men in jail when cosmic conditions freed them]. The jailer turns to these men because they had shown a confidence in hope. While they sang, the other prisoners have

listened. But their conversations had proved them worthy of being heard. [that's why folk don't listen to some of us; our lives and lips tell different stories]. [saved/lie][love/hate][give/stingy][trust/can't][present/absent][Lord's advice/other]

- Paid tribute. He honored the men of God [something I seldom see @ Faith]. The jailer came trembling and fell down before Paul and Silas. Most of you want to be honored yourselves. I need to call your names. Put you on program. Thank you publicly. I pray for you and you refuse to follow me. [children/starve][counsel you on marriage/ill] [home/destroy mine][health/kill me] [give/keep].

What must I do? A question every person has asked a time or two. [marriage][children][home] [job][relationships][government][taxes][bills]. We must come to Jesus with our minds and wills on lasting truth. This is a truly strange and paradoxical situation. Usually the prisoners, not by he that keeps prisoners, ask this question. But with God all things are possible for those that believe.

Closing: So Paul gives this man the answer to life's greatest question. We just simply believe. The word believe means to accept without total evidence. When all seems lost, we need to believe.

- Knowing we are not right with God but trusting a Savior for divine mercy.
- Accepting Him as a friend to whom we can give our hearts.
- Move closer to the Lord to whom we can dedicate our lives.
- Show sincerity of conversation.
- Offer hospitality to those you once treated like an animal.
- Learn more about Christ and put it to good use to draw others to Him.
- Befriend all ambassadors to Christ.

What must you do to be saved? Surrender your self to Christ

- A business woman [Lydia]
- Damsel of divination [ventriloquist]

- Paul and Silas [beaten] [arrested][mistreated]
- Jesus [surrendered self][beaten][arrested][mistreated] but said "Father, forgive them.....

Sermon – Man's Decisions
In The Master's Plan
Acts   Chapter XV   verses 35-41

<u>Introduction</u>: Note the actions of children as they try to persuade parents to do/ buy/get what they want. Or adults that attempt to manipulate others so they too can have their way. It does not matter if they are leaders in the Church of plain pew warmers, few of us will rarely admit it, but we like to have things our way. Check our seniors [excuses], the aged [advice/respect], young adults [time for themselves], youth [peer pressures], children [seek attention], men and women alike [all want to have you listen to them]. But they are usually too busy to listen to you.

Even when the concern is for the Church they seldom believe it [selfish]. Even when the issue is the leadership and headship of God, and trust in a Creator is at stake, most of us still want things to go our way. For some strange reason, most folk really believe they know what's best for everybody else. Examples: They know what Pastors ought to do. [put some out][call others][support some][join these][stay away from those][mean well][don't mean you any good]. In truth, most people seek control, fame, popularity, honor, looked up to, and really would prefer you don't make a move until you hear from me.

A very small number of Churchgoers are truly concerned about Kingdom-building. Most just come when they feel like it [work/bills/chores]. Most just give when they have much [bills/gas]. They want the Light Company to stay in business but the Church can go out of business. They will visit the sick only if they liked the sick before the sick got sick. Or, they will visit the sick if the sick visited them when they were sick. They will offer to help those they like. Or, they will offer to help those that helped them when they needed help. That is not Christ like. We need to love those that hate us and do good for those that despise us, and even pray for those that despitefully use us. We speak up for relatives and friends. But we get angry when others show care for their family and friends. And even here at our Church are classic cases of man's decisions.

1-Prayer. 2-Support. 3-Auxiliaries. 4-Bible-study. 5-Sunday-school. 6-Sermons. 7-Contact & Invites. How serious are we? Christ said he would prefer we be either hot or cold. "For if ye be lukewarm [pretentious; hardly; inconsistent; hard to figure] I will spit you out". But I guess we must remember, "Man was made out of the dust; and when dust gets stuck on itself, it turns to mud".

Here is a passage about 2 great friends. Friends that had endured tremendous hardships together. These men had gone through trouble so enormous that their bond should have been cemented forever. If you get beat together for the cause of Christ, it seems that you ought to stick together for that same cause. When both knew that attacks on their persons were a result of Satan's efforts to stop the growth and grace of the Gospel, they should have gotten along better when matters of disagreement arose. But somewhere in this passage is a lesson for Faith today. For the great causes of God's word, battles are won and lost depending on God's guidance. We never know how what we face, win, and lose will work on the overall plan of salvation. Be the best for God.

<u>Eager to Aide Eternity</u>: The passage tells us that both friends were preachers, called by God [both saved]. They had started so well. On their 1st missionary journey, they had developed a number of Churches throughout the European continent and were eager to revisit them a second time. They knew that time erodes faith [promises; vows; love; trust]. They knew that we as believers must be frequently encouraged [talk good about each other; avoid speaking unfavorably]. We should be eager to aide eternity [testimonies; thankful; offers of help; forgiving].

<u>Positions create Problems</u>: The passage tells us that each man thought he knew best. In verse 37 we see that Barnabas desired that John Mark accompany them on this 2nd missionary journey. But in verse 38, we see where Paul refused to believe the young man merited another chance. [Mark, Barnabas' nephew had deserted them on an island of Pathos [challenged by a soothsayer when sought by a ruler]. Paul never deliberately backslid [makes forgiveness difficult]. The Bible tells the whole story of Paul [birth, training, wealth, family, and heritage]. Paul had special talents [smart; educated; born rich; disinherited; hard-worker, even for the wrong causes; converted; writer of 16 letters] some say he was the 2nd greatest preacher, next to Jesus. But even he lets earthly intellect get in the way of divine designs.

Barnabas had come up different than Paul. He was a Levite that was born with very little. Although he too had worked hard, he had puller himself up by that solid effort. He had a great sense of honesty. He could be trusted. Although he never won the lottery, he did accumulate some property, and sold it when times were hard for the Church and took the money and laid it at the feet of the Apostles. The record says he took no vacation, had very little schooling, but thanks God he had a great deal of common sense. Mark was his nephew and he took up for his relative, thinking he deserved another chance [we all deserve another chance]. Before you think bad about Barnabas, let me tell you what his Biblical resume says. A good man; full of faith.

These men in some ways seemed complete opposites. In others, they seemed just alike. Yet God uses both of them to accomplish His purposes [saving souls]. Barnabas went to Tarsus and secured Paul's help in training the Church @ Antioch [was not too big to seek help]. He spoke up for Paul when others questioned his presence at the conference. Barnabas attested to Paul's sincerity when the disciples worried that he had come to do them harm [risked his reputation for Paul]. Man's decisions in the Master's plan.

<u>God Works It All for Good</u>: We seldom see all that God is doing for us at the time He does it. The Bible has a complete history of how God works things together for good when it involves His purpose. Sampson. Hebrew Boys. Daniel. Joseph. Jesus @ Cross.

Here we have 2 missionary teams rather than just one. Converts could hear the Gospel twice as fast as before. The patience of the relative [Barnabas] developed Mark for future work in the Kingdom. Paul chose Silas [tact; sympathy; manager]. Silas had dual citizen-ship [like Paul]. They could cross certain borders that were prohibited to Paul and Barnabas. Borders [preach to reach the lost; hurting; destitute; broken; blind; etc]. Silas conveyed the 1st Epistle of Peter to Asia Minor, while Barnabas remained in Corinth.

<u>Closing</u>: First, we need to consider the Master's plan [to save every man]. Man's decision is like a dream that is taken by God and made into a reality for faith. Paul meets and trains Timothy [learns patience with youth]. Paul discovers certain things that he never knew about the human spirit [weaknesses; impulsiveness]. Later, Paul sends for Mark [in 2nd Tim. He asks Timothy to bring him to Rome]. Man's decisions have always been used in the Master's plan. Story of Joseph and his brothers. Only God knew that a famine was coming. "You meant it for bad, but the Lord meant it for good".

Sermon – Having Been With Jesus
Acts IV: verses 13-16

<u>Introduction</u>: It is a strange thing to see what a few days does for men. The holidays make men joyous but the debt will make men mad [too much food/fools, gifts/bills]. [King-assassinated] In just a few days [rich-poor][broken romances leads to dreams][winners-losers][respect-shame]. This passage sheds light on the fact that certain men had been with their Master. It showed a difference in behavior that was hard to overlook. It could be seen by all. Noticeable change had taken place, and even those that disliked them had to admit that Jesus created new men of these men. And, I wonder, if men could look at your life, would they know that you kept company with Jesus? Maybe you started wrong [denied], bragged [Peter said, "I will never deny you"], but became disheartened [things did not go like you planned].

Just a few days have elapsed between Peter's denial and Jesus' death. Less than 2 months border the front days of doubt and the back days of belief. These events manifest the grace of God. 51 days earlier, Peter had disowned Christ (believing, trusting, hoping) but a life-changing experience molds Peter's fear into a remarkable courage. In Peter's actions we ought to see ourselves [talk] but when the heat was on [self] somehow the real turn to Christ is seen, even by men in this world. What could have made this difference? There should be something that forms the basis of the foundation of our character. For Peter it was the resurrection. As the investigation went on, the questioners looked for some evidence that produced this calm affect and bold reply. Education? [Peter and John had knowledge of the sea]. Skills and talents [they knew of ropes and nets]. Their looks [rough exteriors and faces of weather-beaten men]. Their station in life? [they had no official capacities]. But you could tell, they had been with Jesus.

<u>What a Christian Ought To Be</u>: Imagine holding cloth close to see if they match. Imagine holding us up to the light to see if we are like Him. There ought to be a <u>striking resemblance of Jesus</u> within us if we really know Him. Instead there is an abundance of professors and protesters. We should yield the right-of-way [not for law but for the gospel]. There ought to be <u>boldness [holy]</u> where we refuse falsehoods for the truth. If we have been purchased, we are debtors. Jesus went back to Nazareth [wanted to make a good impression on the home folk] but talked about widows in Zarapath @ Elijah's day; Syrian soldier [Naaman] with leprosy and Elisha. <u>Understanding</u>, they were without understanding [gnashed their teeth]. <u>Forgiving</u>, from the cross He asked for their forgiveness. <u>Loving</u>, real love for one another [description as disciples]. <u>Concern for others</u>. [children-widow @ Sidon-paralytic-lepers] always for others. <u>Humility</u>. Left Heaven for earth. A man of the poor [ate-lived-sought]. <u>Holy</u>. Ever doing good. Returning good for evil. Submitting to the Father's will.

<u>When We Ought to Be a Christian</u>: Most folk thing it only important to do good on Sunday. We cannot imagine being a Christian on weekdays. [difficult][other folk are not right]. We think we are soldiers on R & R. But what about Christianity @ death's door? We should be an image of Christ <u>@ the house of prayer</u>. (Sunday, Wednesday) But we are too busy for God yet we get angry when He is too busy for us. <u>Even in public</u>. Most of our lives are lived in public. [work; watched in the neighborhood; grocery store; traffic; words; relationships; before our children; paying our bill; paying our tithes]. Even @ home. Who best can judge you as a Christian? Those that live with you. [servants; children; spouse; friends; co-workers]. Even in private. [When no eye except the eye of God sees your motives and your moves]. If our inner lives are written in God's book and He exposes it to all to see, what then is said? [Woman @ the well]. Could we stand the scrutiny?

<u>Why We Ought to Be Like Christ</u>: Realize that God gave Jesus as a pattern for men. History had shown that man went by what he thought rather than by a visible image to copy. Jesus came and said, "now that I have come, men are without an excuse". <u>For their own sakes</u>. Enjoy the benefits of communion with Christ. [Peter walked on water][caught a fish without bait][caught fish when obedient]. We are most unhappy when apart from Christ. <u>For religion's sake</u>. Religion is often injured by foes but frequently is wounded by friends. Church-folk talk about church-folk. [Rome did not bother Jesus much [Pharisees, Scribes, Sadducees, Priests]. <u>For Christ's sake</u>. We need to present Jesus to the world in a way they will believe his words. Have they made a difference in us? [They see no change in us] [walk][talk][cheap][cheat][fight back][seek limelight][want to boss]. But in our lives, they can see his hands [nails] feet [spikes] and his side [wounds] and his brow [thorns]. His scars make us behave differently. His forgiveness makes us forgive. His love makes us love. But we have no proof we have ever been with Him.

<u>How Ought We to Be</u>: We cannot imitate that which we know not. You cannot be like Jesus if you do not know Jesus. You will be a fax [not real], a copy [not real] a photo [not real] look like Him [but not like Him]. <u>Get to Know Jesus</u>. [problems-pains-issues of life]. <u>Be a sacrifice for others</u>. [not selfish][sincere][seeking to put others above yourself]. Not false [fakes on Sundays], bothered by the least little thing. Unstable [like the man that builds on a dream]. <u>Study His character.</u> [see how he handled burdens][watch what he did when life tripped Him][notice how he addressed those that did Him wrong]. <u>Seek His spirit</u>. [wanted no reputation][did not seek the limelight]. We will not come to church to worship but participate on program. <u>Be clothed in His righteousness</u>. [be kind even to those that are unkind to you]. We prefer to be strong [meek seems weak]. <u>Stop worrying about the world's constitution</u>. [His ways are past man's finding out].

<u>Closing</u>: Our lives ought to be a living epistle for all to read and learn about the Lord. The truth is that many of us are fools. We never want to do for Jesus what we ask Jesus to do for us. We are also blind. We see how He changes the lives of

others but refuse to believe He can do it to us too.

So remember that at Heaven's gate sits an angel that recognizes Jesus. As men try to enter, the angel sees inconsistencies in the patterns and denies entry.

- Man with a crown [earthly elevation does not help in Heaven]
- Fame and fortune [earthly gains does not help one gain Heaven]
- Gown of literature and learning [ignorant about the Lord]
- Fair and beautiful [he looks at the heart]
- Poor and illiterate [mistreated-despised-humble] allowed entry

Story of the man that becomes a dog to fix the problems of the dog. Left his nature, family, children, hobbies, diet, and comfort, all.

Sermon – A Choir In The Nursery
Luke II verses 12-15

<u>Introduction</u>: If you have ever been present when a baby is born, one constant you recognize is the quiet zone around the nursery. It is believed that noise interrupts the safe haven sought by the newborn. And noise breaks the rest required by the new mother as she attempts to regain her strength. So it is unusual for us to see a choir singing in the nursery. The one exception we note is when it celebrates the birth of our Savior.

This choir is made up principally with angels. It is superstitious to worship them but proper to love them. Paul warned men against falling down before them but we do need to give them a place of warmest adoration as we consider their work in the lives of believers. They accompanied Christ and attended to his suffering after being tempted by Satan. They came to address his needs just prior his arrest that awful Thursday night before the terrible Friday morning of the cross. And even though they are seen several times when crisis arose, they dip into our memory here to sing a song of praise about the birth of our Master.

But if we could for just a moment, let us look at their character.

- Deeds of sympathy [work with lowly, down trodden, humble, needy, poor]
- Free from envy [Satan took a third from Heaven] Christ took on flesh to redeem man.
- Proud to praise Christ [although they see him different on earth than in Heaven].
- Free from pride [not ashamed to speak about Jesus to common folk].

In song that night, they sang to men of low estate about a king from glory. But if you look @ us.

We prefer to hum along from the pew @ church. But if it is a special occasion, we want to stand @ the microphone. We show no sympathy to those in need @ church. We sit quiet and refuse to speak at our church, but let us go to another church and be asked to give a response. We are too proud to visit the prison and the nursing home; but just let us get an invitation to the White House. Let the king call [up and coming][high and mighty][rich and famous][selected and elected]. We cannot find time to practice [too busy] but let the boss call.

These angels stretched their willing wings and gladly sped from the brightest seats in Heaven to form the chorus in a nursery of unlikely fashion. And just as unexpectedly, a multitude of the heavenly host joined them [best][splendid] [upper crust][those that knew God][waitresses-waiters] left home in glory to worship Christ. Message for us today [we won't leave home][we stay in our comfortable beds][refuse to go out of our way][scared we will lose friends][worried how folk will see us][what will they say]. But here are angels and hosts with spirits that are holy and perfect ministering to us in all facets of life, coming to sing a song of praise to Him that deserves all of our praise.

Instructive: These angels sand something that men could understand [salvation] that gives glory to God. Redemption restores the relationship of care we foster with him when saved. These angels had witnessed God fashion creation [planets][stars][rivers][mountains][seasons][man]. So they knew about his majesty, power, and dominion. These angels gave instruction about the coming child [he would bring peace]. They had been at the garden but did not sing there. They had been with Jacob as he struggled to gain his footing and faith on his way to Bethel, but they did not sing there. They were singing here in the manger that serves as a nursery for the finest infant the world will ever know. They instructed us regarding good will towards men [cursers] [drunks][thieves][murderers][gossipers][busy-bodies][prostitutes][quitters][sinners].

Emotional: This song should stir up our hearts with happiness. This song should develop a deep fellowship with feelings of joy.
- Let us enter his courts with thanksgiving
- Let us come before his altar with praise
- Come boldly before his throne
- The joy of the Lord is my strength.

Prophetic: These angels prophesied that we should give glory to God in the highest sense possible. For the great things he has done. [supplied needs][answered prayers][satisfied all of our longings][addressed our greatest desires][calmed all our doubts and fears]. But do we see God honored among men? What we see is the heathen bowing down before idols [cars][clothes][cash]. Tyranny seems to be lording over men causing us to look beyond God. He seems to be forgotten. Men are chasing money. But the angels said there would be peace on earth. Yet we live in discord rather than harmony [home-jobs-schools-church-relationships-banks-businesses-life]. The clarion call for war even affects our good will towards men. We worry that someone might be getting ahead of us. So good will is only known as a store, not an extension of man's concern for man.

So today, man has X'd out the word Christ from Christmas. He is the center of all things but missing from our celebration. Instead of glory to God, we seek it for ourselves. Instead of peace on earth, we live with the smell of war as the fragrance of existence. Instead of good will to men, we rather do good for things rather than for persons. So the angels have come to the nursery to lift our hopes in song.

Amid the nasty animals and the dirty stable, lies the most precious gift ever given. But we are too busy to join in the chorus. We are filled with excuses about rehearsal. We are angry that about who leads the song. But all angels have joined with the host to form a wonderful choir. Because the center of celebration demands that we forget who gets the glory.

Sermon - Good News For
The Common Man
Luke II verses 8-11

<u>Introduction</u>: Patience [virtue] Waiting is the mark of a man that trusts God for his resources. But in this passage we find a world that had waited so long. For over 400 years, they had listened for the voice of God and it had remained silent. Malachi, the prophet had been the last to tell men what God said. And when Malachi talked, the Babylonians had overtaken the Assyrians. The Greeks [Alexander] had overthrown the Babylonians. The Romans had overthrown the Greeks and it was indeed a brand new world. Crisis loomed on every corner. Danger lurked at every turn. Lies filled the pulpit. Preachers were sending men to hell. The priests were telling men that there was no life after death. It is believed that men made fun of the truth God had relayed to Job [if a man die, shall he live again?]. So the news was bad for the rich man; worse for the common man.

Into this condition steps the body of a baby. It caused great trouble for those in power. An angelic message of comfort and hope stills the uncertainty of Zechariah and Elizabeth. It produced a trust in the unknown for the virgin, Mary. It satisfied the worry of the "soon-to-be" husband, Joseph. It brought great news for the common man [shepherds]. It brought a political message [taxes]. God uses events for eternity. This birth [stable-hospital] [donkey-doctor][rags-royalty][bread @ feeding trough][lamb @ manger]. Good news!

<u>The End of Fear</u>: [*angels brought 2 words of comfort; fear not*] These shepherds were really common men [history] and very afraid. But the thread of Biblical cloth identifies fear as a common emotion [Adam/Eve sin][Abraham lied about Sarah][Jacob & Esau] [Moses faced Pharaoh and rejection][Israel @ Promised land]. Fear stalked mankind throughout the centuries but Jesus would move about in man's world and quiet his fears. [disciples in storms][blind Bartimaeus][10 lepers afraid][Mary & Martha – Lazarus] [Peter denies Christ][Thomas @ Samaria][men @ death's door] worried.

We too are worried. Even though it's Christmas, we worry [jobs][health][economy] [world conditions with Saddam & bin Laden][politics][family][children] [marriage][life]. But Jesus brings faith to combat the fear [saved by faith][restored by faith][kept by faith] that is good news for the common man.

<u>The Birth of Joy</u>: [*bring you good tidings (news) of great joy*]. The songs at Christmas are about joy [do you hear what I hear?][silent night][hark the herald][little town of Bethlehem][joy to the world].

- A savior has been born [our birth].
- Scripture has been fulfilled [what does the bible say

about us?]
- ■ Our Lord and King has been given to us [what shall we give?]

<u>The Start of Evangelism</u>: [*which shall be to all people*] Up to this time, all news had been to the fortunate [rich][royalty][respected][renown]. But God fixed it so that regular folk could receive the good news [shepherds][sad][sinners][scared][simple]. Not knowing all about God was no longer an excuse. All men needed a savior.

- ■ Romans II:23 "all have sinned and come short"
- ■ Romans V: 8 "by one man death came and by one man salvation came".

He is available for the common man [shepherds]. But his birth brought uncommon changes. Look at their activities with good news [affected politics][brought angels from Heaven][summoned the Heavenly host][affected worshippers] [beckoned wise men from afar][accompanied by stars] [confounded scholars] [revealed trickery][made exiles of a King].

Christmas is a depressing time for most folk [emotional crisis][drink][overeat] [leave work][no school][spend $][rowdy][robbing][suicides][break ups][etc.]

But everywhere we look, we see His name. While he is on man's mind, we ought to speak up for him [wino][sluggard][prostitute][beggar][sick & infirmed][homeless][hopeless][helpless][liar] [cheater][gambler][brother][sister][father][mother][lost][diseased][backslider][murmurers].

Spread the word. [Unto us this day, is born in the city of David, Christ the Lord]. Sin-free.

Sermon – Moving From Anger To Restraint
Proverbs Chapter-29 verses 9-11

<u>Introduction</u>: One day a preacher was traveling to attend a conference in another city. Decided to take his 5-year daughter with him. Like most children, she asked a lot of questions. Over and over, she asked "are we there yet?" He got slightly angry after awhile. So he told her to go to sleep and when she woke up they should be closer to their destination. After 5 minutes, she woke up and asked again, "Are we there yet?" The preacher said, with anger in his voice "no, we are not there yet but we are almost there". She then said, if we are not there yet, where are we? He said to her I don't know where we are but I know we are almost there!

Her next words are truly prophetical in their use for spiritual application. She muttered under her breath to avoid making daddy more angry.."if you don't know where we are, how do you know we are almost there? That phrase is good for a little girl to say when feeling lost. But it means so much more to those that are trying to make their way to Heaven. It stretches out across the landscapes of history for children trying to get promoted and graduate. It jumps out for the spouse that tries to do more for their partner. How can you know what to do if you don't know what you have already done? How close are we to Heaven if we don't know where Heaven is? Having never been there before, how do we know how close we are?

Many Christians think they are almost there. Just about perfect but never recognizing they are lost, as the preacher seemed to his little girl. Church folk, that leave believing they are doing right but lift no fingers to help those that are in need. They never bend their knees to pray for the sick, the infirmed, the starving, the homeless, the hopeless, and even the helpless. A lot of Christians are filled with <u>anger</u> [rejection, baby but no husband, educated & unemployed]. Others just simply have a bad <u>attitude</u> [fear, not honored, want their name called, not promoted]. Still there are those that belong in royalty because they are <u>drama queens</u> [acting, magnifying all problems and solutions]. Finally, there are also folk in church that require <u>high maintenance</u> [need attention all the time, got to beg them to join].

American surveys show that 7 out of 10 Americans are on the verge of exploding. Rage is just on the lip of falling from the mouth of the most calm person [airline passengers, drivers, schools, actors, soccer fields]. It seems that Christians have forgotten the words or have lost our trust in the Lord's words "vengeance is mine, I will repay". We have a natural urge to take matters into our own hands. Our tongues, without a single bone in them, having not bullets or sticks, cause more pain and problems that all the guns in the world. But if we are going to move from anger to restraint we need God's help, God's love, and God's guidance.

Test: Line @ the grocery store. Fast lane on the freeway. Anger [finger, words, wishing worse]. My personal story about something my wife said to me or something someone decided not to do for me. It really ticked me off. But what do we do when angry? How are we supposed to handle it when folk go against our wishes? Look into the Bible to see how other men of God handled it.

Point No-1: *Stop overestimating yourself* [foolish]. People think they are all that. [looks, smarts, @ work, @ home, @ church, family]. Folk do not have to have you. You need to work to fit in [too many of us just accept facts we tell ourselves "they just don't like me, they don't want me]. Drama queens act out parts that require attendance and applause [clapping, paying attention, it is always worse than it really is] Story of chicken little and 'the sky is falling'.

Point no-2: *Things will not always go your way* [foolish]. Too many folk think that the world should stop and let them go by. [children-best; looks-greatest; car-park; voice-better; speak-well; know-more; kiss-sweetest; walk-look; late-but we need to be glad they came; important-cannot do without them]. We need to know things will not always go our way. Story of Joseph and brothers. Some days will start one way, but will end another way. [job-fired; doctor-sick; court-jail; married-divorce; credit card-revoked; group-put out].

Point No-3: *Give it a Rest* (Whatever the problem, past, pain) give it a rest. Verse-9 says that a fool never lets it rest. We spot the person that is really wrong when we see they cannot forgive [story of Peter questioning Jesus about forgiving his brother 7 times]. Envy in there somewhere. Note our anger with the person in the grocer line in front of us. There are folk behind us with just as many items or more. They even have a check. But we are not angry with them. They are behind us. There is a little jealousy in there too. There are persons going slow in the fast lane that is in back of us. But we are not mad with them. Why? Because they are behind us. We only get mad with folk in front of us.

Point No-4: *The problem rests inside not outside*. There is nothing wrong with the person in line with too many items. There is something wrong with you. There is nothing wrong with the person going slow in the fat lane. There is something wrong with you. Stop saying somebody made you mad. Can't nobody make you mad, but you. If the cashier waited on you, even if you had too many items, you would be glad. If you see a wreck and the only lane is the fast lane, you want the right to go through in the fast lane, even though you go through slow [looking @ wreck].

Point No-5: *We fail to Appreciate*. [Be thankful that we can do what we do]. The person going slow may be scared, may not see well, and may be sick. Well, they should not be driving. May be there is nobody else to take them to the hospital. The person in the grocery line with too many items may not be able to write [count] and the cashier is their sister who will write the check or count the money without cheating them. Question-have you almost had a wreck? Do you know the number of cars God slowed down to help you avoid that collision? Sped up? That was designed before you were ever born. "For we know that all things work together for the good of those that love God and are called according to his purpose".

If you are going to move from anger to restraint you need to;
- Stop taking life so seriously [learn to laugh].
- Quit trying to intimidate people [words or pen or possessions].
- Enjoy this Journey [it ends too soon] Job said this life is too short and filled w/trouble.

Christians that want to move from anger to restraint need to know where they are, even if they are not there yet. Adopt some standards for your life [God's rules work just fine]. Keep your faith. Practice restraint by controlling your tongue. In plain language, watch your words!
- Torn down more kingdoms.
- Destroyed more relationships.
- Got more folk fired from their jobs.
- Stops church growth.
- Hinder those that are Heaven bound.

Sermon-The Only Reliable Deposit Insurance

Matthew Chapter-6 Verses 19-21

Introduction: Back during a period called the Roaring-20's, America enjoyed what was known up and until that time as the Great Prosperity. [ban on booze-prohibition-bootleggers-illegal gains-made rich men][garment industry-cloth squeeze-imports-rich men][WWI-need for housing-rich men][soldiers-married-houses-jobs-cars-Ford-rich men][endless game called supply/demand][rich got richer, separation grew among citizens, and the thought was that it would not end].

But in 1929, the Stock Market crashed [Great Depression][run on banks][loan defaults][land deals went sour][business failures][private schools closed][banks failed][raining bodies on Wall Street][soup lines formed][families moved in with one another][bank robbers Dillinger/Nelson/ Floyd/Ma Barker/Bonnie & Clyde]. But out of that era came 2 fantastic government-sponsored departments. The country elected a new President [FDR] brought a new cabinet [Treasury-FDIC] and opened the State [FBI]. It slowed economic growth but it stabilized banks. It threatened man's global security but it made a man's money safe. [treasure-root of all evil]. So this AM, I want to remind us all of practicing care in treasures, deposits, and insurance.

Jesus did not oppose your having a treasure. [treasure chests][treasure hunts] [treasure island]. But in His introduction to the new Kingdom [Sermon-on-the-Mount] He strives to give the character of those that would make up the citizenship. "You can't be wrong and belong". Christians are like the foreigners [sinners]-immigrate [saved]-prefer [choose]-study/learn [Bible]-abide [obey]-oath [promise service]-enjoy benefits [King]. He recognizes that you must have a treasure. He even gives us here, direction about the only secure place to deposit our treasures. It is our choice to select where we will put our best. Either in a place where it will perish or a place where it is preserved. When Jesus used the term treasure, He did not mean a great hoard of wealth. In His world a treasure was a slight margin, anything left over from subsistence. So for those of you that think only those with a bank account are to be warned. I am talking to folk today that have a car to be sold [walking] or with furniture [auctioned] or clothes [sold] TV-cable/paper/eating-out/ buying new items/trusting jobs/relationships/health. All those things may be your treasures.

<u>Having Treasures:</u> In v-19, the Lord begins with a prohibition. "Do not lay up for yourselves treasures on earth". He detected and attitude that he wanted to discourage. Disciples argued about rank [church-folk]. Many wanted to make money in a protected society [no taxes]. He warned against storing up treasures that are only for yourselves [stingy/selfishness/ covetousness] He further gives

an explanation. Every earthly treasure is transient. In that primitive, simple society there were no pantries, storehouses, banks, safes, and police. Treasures were kept @ home in the form of garments, foodstuff, and precious metals. Each of these had its' own enemy. Some enemies were impersonal. Moths ate heirlooms. Mold destroyed foods. Corrosion ate away precious metals. But then too, there were personal enemies. Thieves could dig under the mud walls and steal treasures. And although treasures and enemies may have been different in Jesus' day, the truth still remains the same. No treasure on earth is safe.

Jesus does not prohibit saving and planning [rainy days]. God gives the power to collect wealth [Abraham-Job-David]. God expects us to save [Prov; 21:20]. He even directs us to the ant to learn to set aside something for the future. Parents ought to provide for their children [future]. What Jesus forbids is our giving primary intensity to treasures on earth. He warns against the attitude of excess [cars/homes/clothes/jewelry/food/money]. We should govern our treasures, not be governed by our treasures. In Samaria, he met the woman @ well; food – God's will.

Heavenly Treasures: Jesus then points to a reality. You can have a treasure in Heaven. His command is to start now investing in a Heavenly business. How? You cannot launch your funds into space. There is no armored car that can fly into the pearly gates. So the idea is to deposit your treasures in heaven by allowing the right use of your possessions on earth [Kingdom-building]. You can invest in this age and meet the needs you have in the ages to come.
You deposit treasures in heaven when you support those who are in need. Jesus said even when you give a cup of water to those in need [in His name], you building heavenly treasures. In fact, Luke 16:9 tells me that if I allow my resources to be used for aid for others, that when I get to heaven, they will be there to greet me. So let us deposit our treasures by putting it to work in the lives of those that are going there. It will be secure [no impersonal/personal enemies can threaten In Heaven the market never varies. In Heaven the value of the dollar never changes. In Heaven the GNP is balanced. Only what you give to Christ will last.

Hearts' Treasures: Nobody had the insight that Jesus has into the human heart. Jesus understood it all too well. He had made so many. [cries/worried/love for children/concerns for future] So when you really look at it, the real reason Jesus told us where to put our treasures has everything to do with our hearts. "For where your treasures are, there your hearts will be also". Solomon said "my heart pants after her presence. Sunflowers grow in the direction of the sun. The compass needle like a magnet follows the sun. A boy goes every evening to the love of his lady. So too must our hearts flow heavily after our treasures.

The Biblical definition of heart represents the very center of your personality. [intellectually, emotionally, willingly] Our heart goes where our money goes [church/hospital/club/organization] when we put all our investments into this world; our hearts are captured by this world. But when you put your money in the works of the Lord, your hearts are captured by the Lord. Excuses have no place in His presence [Christ called…married/oxen/father and mother]. Our church could use the work of your heart. That work is exciting, successful, and true. _Cars_ [no eating] _homes_ [no freedom] _jobs_ [no missing] _children_ [no effort] _money_ [no loaning/giving] _attitudes_ [no leaving]. When you see how much folk care about the church, what you see is how much they give to the church. [time-talent-tears]

One of every six verses in the Gospels deals with a man's relationship with money. We handle our money more than any other commodity of life. When we face God, we will see the CPA [Christian Production Accountant] or the FA [faith in action]. But one way or another, we will all give an account of our stewardship. The FDIC is only guaranteed to shore deposits when there is economic upheaval. In the event of war, America must use its' resources to fight and defend. Its' that same way with Heaven's army. Since we fight against an unseen enemy, all resources must be used for soldiers. Are you a soldier in the army of the Lord?

Story of the Rabbi and the rich man [glass, mirrors, silver, others only ourselves].

Sermon-Trying To Get It Right
Isaiah-Chapter XXXVII-Verses 1-7

<u>Introduction</u>: One of the things we can be sure about in this life is the effort we must make trying to get things right. If you trust that things are just the way you want them to be, just wait. In a few, short minutes, things will change. [Friendships][Employment][School][Christian walk][Bank accounts][Dreams][Marriages][Child-rearing]. And although we fail, what we seek is another chance to get it right. Politicians seek another term in office [admitting failure in their earlier terms]. Mistakes in relationships find us asking, begging for another chance [because we see poor practices in the earlier acts]. Job hunters promise themselves they will make better employees if they get another job [discover their lackadaisical attitude brought them dismissal]. Often, we take things for granted and make the mistake of trusting that folks have to have us. But only to wake up one day, find that significant thing/person is gone and them we start trying to get it right.

This passage is about a King [Hezekiah] that started out good. Got filled with pride and saw things falling apart and now seems to be trying to get it right. Earlier in his career, this king had purged and repaired the Temple @ Jerusalem [neglected and polluted by his father, Ahaz]. He had rooted out Canaanite fertility gods and cut down the high groves as well as destroyed the brazen serpent used by Moses in the wilderness to rid the people of snakes [it had become an idol]. Devil uses things God blesses us with to make idols for us [cars, clothes, careers, children, cottages, comforts]. But Hezekiah restored the Passover and Israel enjoyed a refreshing time of peace and joy from the Lord. Hezekiah had worked to strengthen the spiritual, moral, agriculture, trade, and defensive positions of the nation. So he had made a good start. But along the way, he had gotten lifted up in pride and lost his trust of God. Somehow, he saw all that he had and thought it would continue forever. [Us, today]. He formed an allegiance with Egypt [world] and trusted that if trouble came, Egypt would come to his rescue. [Us, today (bank accounts; jobs; spouses; homes; insurance]. But God had helped Sennacarib to defeat Egypt and that left Hezekiah all alone.

The passage starts after Assyria had sent a message to Hezekiah that they were going to destroy Israel and take him captive. He is worried but first thing he does is rends his clothes. Rids himself of anything that might stand between him and God. He covers himself with sackcloth and ashes to express his self-humiliation and grief. He sends the news of the threat to the Prophet Isaiah [preacher] and asks for prayer. His dignity is forgotten as "he humbles himself before the mighty hand of God & He will exalt you in due time". We are more familiar with the verse that says, "cast all your cares upon Him, for He cares for you".

Sennacarib had not only overthrown Egypt, but also the Philistines, Moabites, and the Edomites. He had a mighty army and was ruthless in his attacks. So fear was natural. Cancer has defeated a many man. But it has never defeated God. I care not how difficult it may be for you this morning; you need to try to get it right. King Hezekiah sent a contingent of ambassadors to the Prophet. Eliakim, his chief steward; Shebna, the scribe [record-keeper] and chief financial officer; and the elders of the priests. The priests had been his major confidants, but he could not trust their advice any longer.

We know our lives and recognize that we are undeserving of God's help. In verse 3 we discover more about the profound agitation Hezekiah suffered. He saw victory as certain for his enemy. His words are "this day" [amazing thing about a day] trouble. [starts one way and ends another [work/unemployed][well/sick] [rich/broke][married/divorced][alive/dead]. The day was also one of rebuke. Ambassadors from Assyria had slipped in undetected and that scared Hezekiah. Things can come upon us undetected [disease; change in relationships; loss of jobs; backsliding]. This day was also one of blasphemy. Sennacarib had claimed to win in spite of the Lord's assistance. That was a lie. He counted his successes and thought soon I will have it all. In his personal chronicles, this heathen king said "the Jew refuses to bow down before me, even though I have taken his people [200,000], 46 walled cities, daughters [drugs], his wives [illness], choirs [quit], jewels [sell], livestock [too many to count] and caged him up like a bird in Jerusalem [Holy City]".
Sennacarib makes the grave mistake of counting his chickens before they hatch. It may seem late, but you can still get it right. In the f-clause of verse-3, Isaiah states the problem in a gynecological term. He says that Israel is like a pregnant mother whose child is now at term [ready for deliverance] but the mother is too weak to deliver and the child will die in the womb. Speaking of Judah, he says they are too weak. Militarily [soldiers captured]; physically [their crops had been burned]; financially [jewels and gold was gone]; and spiritually [they had made an alliance with the world]. Some times when our needs are the greatest, our strength fails and we are weak. [sick & broke][debt & out-of-work] [leave church & need the church].

But in verse-4, Hezekiah begins to get it right. He appeals to Isaiah to use his relationship with God. Maybe you have no relationship with God. Maybe the one you got with Him is not good. Maybe the one you had was good but you messed it up. But if you are trying to get it right, start with connecting to somebody that does have a solid relationship with God. The Bible says that "the effectual, fervent prayer of a righteous man availeth much". Hezekiah said, "it may be that God will hear [not notice; not punish] just hear. Knowing God hears us means so much! He cannot hear us cry and do nothing about it. David said, "incline thine ear"; Job said "oh that I might talk with Him to confirm he has heard my call"; we even sing a song that says "pass me not O gentle Savior, hear my humble cry". Just to be heard. Hezekiah wanted the words of the infidel listed before God. Sennacarib [Devil] Rabshakeh [representative]; your enemy (whatever it is-Devil] your situation [representative]. He refers to God as the living God [opposed to dead-idols] but lets us in on a secret…why do we think we will lose?

Maybe I am talking to someone here today that started strong, but along the way, you strayed. Maybe somebody or at least something has caused you to lose a little ground [worried about them rather than ourselves] So, pray for us is the request [remnant] a little left [faith-hope-belief-trust-love] That is all we need a little left. They had come to the Prophet thinking it was too late. Is it to late for you??

Listen to God's reply. (1) *Don't be afraid of their threats [words/actions].* (2) *Stop listening to their lies. (3) Get your anger and agitation under control; it's only hurting you.* "Stand still and see the glory of God revealed". God wants to prove to you that he is bigger than your circumstances. Better yet, (4) *do not take matters in your own hands.* "Vengeance is mine, says the Lord, I will repay". God would put a blast [spirit] upon him and remove his arrogance and pride from him. God would replace it with fear and hesitation [driving with confidence]. "He shall hear a rumor" [God uses a rumor-whatever he chooses]. Sennacarib had Jerusalem surrounded [enemies]. It looked like Assyria was winning. Your problems [jobs; debt; children; sickness; companionship; devil] winning. News came to him that someone was after his throne. [Your job; spouse, place]. He had to make a decision keep up the invasion or put down the insurrection. God said.."not only will he leave you alone, but the rumor will make him go back home; where he will die by the sword in his own land. [You will not have to kill him]. Look at verses 37 and 38, where it says he returned to Nineveh and was killed by 2 of his sons.

Story of persistence. Electricity seeks the path of least resistance. Rivers travel around great mountains. We sit in front of TV instead of helping our neighbors. Spouses argue instead of sitting down and talking out the problem. But electricity and water will never have to stand before God and give an account of their service. We will. So, we better get to getting and try to get it right.

Sermon - God Left Him
II Chronicles Chapter-32 verses 27-31

<u>Introduction</u>: One of the greatest sins in mans arsenal of failures is that called pride. You see it often in men after they have scaled high challenges. You see it when men accumulate great wealth and can buy friends and pay to quiet his enemies. You see it when men make much of themselves and pay to still the voices of those that said he would never amount to anything. Pride jumps out at us, even in men that are blessed with God's hand of choice. David, in pride, took Abigail from her husband, when the husband made fun of David, and the King showed him how powerful it was to wear the crown. But it was after David had failed to go to war that he stopped listening to the voice of God. As a result David took census of the people against God's command. God had said that Abraham's offspring would be counted as the sands of the sea [unknown]. And that only He would be able to know how many folk really served God. So, God left David, and David soon found out that his joy was gone the same day the Lord left.

In today's text, we have a man that is also King of Israel by the name of Hezekiah. The record tells us that this man was something special. In the way of special we see <u>his wealth</u>. Verse 27 starts with much wealth. Historians said he resembled Solomon in pay and approached almost $50-M a year (today's standards). Not only did he have a lot, he had it in varied terms and ways. Precious metals of silver, gold, & stone [republican]. Spices for his chef, shields for his army, pleasant jewels for his ladies. He had it all. But God left him.

The record also tells us about <u>his works</u>. It says the man had many large fields that produced great harvests existed and this required huge storehouses. There were horses in abundant and he needed stalls and stables and riders and tenders to care for his herds. Furthermore, he developed cities, or vacation places, with watchtowers and guards for comfort and safety. His dwelling places resembled modern-day hotels with cooling stations and maid quarters so that every detail for life had been looked into for the good of the King. But God left him.

Hezekiah was growing so inwardly great, and priding himself so much upon the favor of God, that self-righteousness crept in. And through his carnal security, the grace of God was withdrawn from its' active operation. Like the landowner in Jesus' parable. Hezekiah forgot who it was that really was responsible for his rise to power. He forgot the name of Him that had turned on the spotlight of time and attention for Israel's good.

But that did not slow the growth of pride. No, no, not in Hezekiah. There was even <u>his walk</u>. You might remember that this same king had one day gotten sick. God, in His infinite mercy, had sent the great prophet by to announce that his sickness was terminal. In those days, folk that loved the Lord did not hear news about their demise from physicians. They did not believe it until the man of God told them. [today?]. But Hezekiah reportedly turned his face to the wall and prayed unto God in such a way as to remind God of his walk. Had he not done what God told him to do? Did not he perform all works unto His glory, for the good of all Israel? Was that not enough to alter the will of God? Evidently! God sent the prophet back again to prescribe the medicine that would heal the king [fig leaves on his boil]. So, at that time, God was with him.

The news of his recovery got out. Rival kings that had heard about his sickness, were waiting, holding their breath in anticipation of his death. All this stuff that he had. They could see themselves with it. If he would just die, they thought a takeover was imminent and riches were within reach. But when they heard about his recovery, they sent emissaries and ambassadors to honor the king for his restoration. [all right, if real]. [shameful, when false]. Upon the arrival of _princes_ from Babylon, Chaldea, and Assyria, king Hezekiah began to demonstrate his wealth. He illustrated his noble deeds. He pointed out those things that had brought him the highest honors. But, he forgot God. Nowhere in his correspondence did he mention how God had brought him out. [severity of his ill] [arrival of the prophet][prayer and its' effects][prophet returns and prescription] [He left God out]. The best wealth is grace. The noblest deeds are our works of faith. The highest honor is salvation and glory. But Hezekiah left God first. [Is there someone here today that has left God?]
Here is enough to account with these Babylonians, Chaldeans, & Assyrians. For if the grace of God should leave the best of Christians, there is enough sin in each of our hearts to make us the worst transgressors. If we are left to ourselves, those of us that are the warmest for Christ will cool down like Peter before the damsel at Pilate's palace when he said.."I know not the man of whom you speak". Those that are sound in the faith would be white with leprosy, affected by the false doctrine of prosperity. Those of us that now walk before the Lord in excellency would reel to and fro, staggering with the drunkenness of evil passion. Like the moon, that borrows its' light from the sun; we borrow our brightness from the righteousness of the Son of God. We are dark by ourselves. Only He brightens us and our pathways. [word-a lamp unto me feet, light-pathways]

But in his splendor of life [prime]. When all was going so well. Hezekiah built a water canal and channeled water from the Gihon spring for his personal exclusivity. [Gihon-spring that fed all of Jerusalem]. Hezekiah's selfishness was rooted in pride. Born as a baby, selfishness grows to be the adolescent of unmerciful behavior. It soon becomes the adult of stinginess and refuses to share things that benefit the masses. Not only had Hezekiah made a great political blunder, he also committed a providential transgression. So the text tells us that God left him. [real issue is trust].

But see here a change in God's way of dealing with Hezekiah. When the king got sick, God warned him in an effort to prepare him for his eventual demise. But because Hezekiah did not honor God's right to do as He pleased with those He made, God altered His methods of bringing Hezekiah down to size. The Bible does not tell us of another warning for this king. While it does tell us the reason for leaving, [to try Hezekiah] (*trust*) it never tells us of a second warning. [dwell on 1st warnings][dwell on 1st coming of Christ].

Therefore, let us cry to God and pled that He never leaves us. I know He promised never to leave us. But sometimes we make Him go away. [disobedient, murmuring, backbiting, troubling, lazy, and stubborn]. David said "please don't take they spirit from me". But one thing I warn us about today. Maybe he won't withdraw from us. But there might be a call among ourselves to withdraw from Him. [disciples asked," where shall we go? You have the gift of eternal life].

Lord, keep us everywhere. Keep us in the valley, that we murmur not against they humbling hand. Keep us on the mountain, that we wax not giddy through being lifted up. Keep us in our youth. When our passions are strong. Keep us in old age. When in danger of conceit from wisdom, we become greater fools than the young, gifted, and proud. Keep us Lord, when we come to die, lest at the very last, we should deny Thee. Keep us living, keep us from dying, keep us laboring, keep us from suffering, keep us fighting, keep us resting, and keep us believing.

Let us learn the lessons in the danger of flattery, the sin of ostentation, the feebleness of good men when left by God, the necessity off having a heart right in relationship with Christ, and the certainty that God does indeed try us all.

Sermon - He Went A Little Farther
Matthew Chapter-XXVI verses 36-39

Introduction: If you could call upon your powers of imagination, you would picture this situation in which Jesus found himself. If you could just think about your selves for a little while, you might understand how he felt on this particular Thursday night. The record reports that it is just about 14 hours before his death. And He, who knows all things, knew death was approaching [hour had come]. Since he died on Friday, a bit after 10:00 in the morning, it is near 8:00 on Thursday night. They had just finished eating what we commonly know as the Last Supper. They had song their closing song. Jesus kept the law fully even unto the very end. His fake friend Judas, has departed and gone to fetch the others that were destined to arrest Him and try Him in night court [violation of Israel & Rome]. He had heard the promises of the disciples that none would desert him. They said that "even if it cost them their lives, they would stick by Him until the bitter end".

Jesus had a custom of praying every night. And He selected a place that lay beneath the shoddy wooden bridge that crossed the Kidron Valley. As the valley descended at the foothills of Mount Olivet, there was a quiet garden where men went to press olives that was used for oil to light men's lamps. Under the bridge that crossed men over, our Lord went to pray. Gethsemane, when crisis came. Sights, sounds, serenity, seclusion was at Gethsemane. Up until that night, this place had been one of peace, rest, and joy. [life]. His friends knew this was the place to which He withdrew. So it is with friends today. That is what made it easy for Judas, he knew the pattern. It is in front of those we trust that we let our guards down. Relax, kick-back, just be self. Drop the professional act, just be down with homey [dog].

So Jesus comes to Gethsemane. Just a few hours before his greatest trial. Just a few days until the dawn of a new generation. But just a few minutes before his arrest. Point No-1 is that all of us have our personal Gethsemane [fragrance-falsehoods][quiet-questions][beauty-betrayal][love of life-loss of life][memory-misery][growth-destruction][rest-refusal][give-gain][death is sealed with a kiss]. Maybe your Gethsemane is a job, problem with health, debt and brokenness, breakup and uncertainty, sickness and old age. But all of us got a Gethsemane. And it is when we come to our personal Gethsemane that we want most to be comforted by our friends.

He took the 11 disciples with him. He motions to those that he felt really followed him to sit while he did the praying. Did not ask them to pray. He would take care of that Himself. He just asked them to sit. Sometimes, we just want our friends & loved ones to be with us. Like the 4 friends that carried the lame man to let him down in the hole in the roof. We will take care of the bill [eat] fare [go] rent [stay] buy [share]. Jesus admits it is required for Him to go a bit farther. [Remind of the story of Abraham and his servants when he went to sacrifice Isaac]. He went a little farther.

But he took a greater distance Peter and the sons of Zebedee. Jesus has allowed Peter, James & John to witness his transfiguration on the mount. He knew that in this day of testing, they would need that experience to withstand the worry and anxiety awaiting their arrival @ Gethsemane. These 3 men had been granted the privilege of seeing Him raise the daughter of Jarius and go through special challenges extended only to those in the inner circle. So although there were others classified as disciples, it was these 3 that He expected to stand with him during this terrible time. [we share great experiences with one another because we expect those significant persons to stand by us, even when errors result from decisions.

Jesus said, my soul, not my body, but the innermost part of my being. It begins to feel heavier than at any time previously. It is so heavy, I am worried about death. [Men always worry about death [Job-Abraham-Saul-Hezekiah-Isaac-John the Baptist, Jesus]. Natural man was created mortal and expects to die. But the first man Adam was made perfect and holy and never thought about death until after his sin. So Jesus, the perfect God-man, knew no sin and could not have worried about death until this night. He had spoken about it on many occasions, but only this night, did he fully understand the pain, agony, fear, ending, and suffering of death. He begged his friends, stay here with me and watch. They did not know the trails that awaited each of them. In a while, they would all disappear, deny, disappoint, and dissolve the close brotherhood they loved.
Wait here with me, just one hour. Isn't that a small request to fill? Hold on for me for 60 minutes. In one hour, I fed 5000. In one hour, I came walking to your on the stormy sea and rescued your weary souls. In just one hour, I gave sight [blind] healed [sick and infirmed] made blind [see] and made dumb [talk]. In just one hour, Judas and the others are coming for me. After that, I won't bother you no more. Have you ever asked your friend [significant other] to just tarry with you for one hour? Put up with me [problem][bother][ask for more than I deserve]. If they only knew how awful they would feel when their Master was gone, they might have not only tarried with him, they might have prayed too. So often, we never know what the next minute will bring. So it is a good idea to just go on a little farther. No matter what the cost, try it again. No matter what others may say, give it another chance.

The 39th verse says that Jesus went a little farther. I don't think men really give this passage its' justice. The collective concepts listed in all 4 gospels tell us that he only walked a stone's throw away from them. But to fully accept the scriptural message on this clause, we need to look at the life of Christ as a whole. In every walk and way, He indeed went a little farther. Although the vast of society did not embrace his teaching, he taught them just the same. Even though they turned their backs on him, he still faced them and aided their every need. In incident after incident, Jesus proved he went above and beyond the call of duty. (woman at well) He went a little farther. (blind Bartemaus) He went a little farther. [lepers] He went a little farther. [Lazarus] He went a little farther.

But when faced with the crisis of life, Jesus prayed. You do not see him planning, plotting, predicting, picking and choosing, running, fuming, fretting, but praying [good idea]. He fell on his face. Did not sit on his hands. Prayed "O my Father". That depends on the relationship we have with God. [if we don't know Him, we have to say my God (general, for everybody)] but [if we really know him, if he made a way for you, you can say My Father]. Jesus, my Father, I know your name [name under the Heavens, whereby men can be saved]. You must break the prayer down. He prayed, "if it be possible" [that means there were things the Father may have kept hidden from Jesus]. Bible readers recall when the disciples asked when the end of the world would come. In response Jesus said, "that secret rests only with the Father". But he also asked, "let this cup pass from me". I hate to tell you this, but there are some cups that God just won't let pass. Some things we have to go through. [sickness, surgery, loss of loved ones, joblessness, separation, trials, jail, and tribulations of every kind]. But Jesus went a little farther.

Down in the verse, you see Him surrender his own, personal feelings for those of God. He says, "nevertheless not as I will, but as thou wilt". That is going a little farther. He yielded his future for the future of all mankind. Bible readers remember that when King Hezekiah got sick. And God sent the prophet to tell him that he was going to die. But Hezekiah turned his face to the wall, and prayed. He begged God to change his will. But not Jesus. He went a little farther.

In love [farther] in care [farther] in praise [farther] in help [farther] in teaching [farther] in life [farther] death [farther] in preparing for us a better place, he is still going farther. In respect for what he did, believers ought to be asking today, what we can do since Jesus went a little farther.

I know I will behave different in the face of danger. I will [believe-doubt]. I will [love-hate]. I will [help-refuse my help]. I will [give-struggling and destitute]. I will [be there-when told to leave]. I will [hope-against all hope]. I will succeed-failure]. I will [when down-get up and try again]. I will [trust-when it seems untrue].

One day there was a small boy in England that spoke with a stutter. While growing up, he was never smart and never made a scholar. When war came to his country, they rejected him because they said he could not speak. When elected to the congress, men walked out of the chambers whenever he rose to speak. But that man kept trying and spoke to empty chairs and an empty chamber. But when the war got heated and England began to lose, that same man spoke of an iron will and the courage to fight until they could fight no more. So today, the world knows him as Winston Churchill. [I am going to hold on, in the face of trial/frustrations/failures].

Sermon - The Pastor with A Servant's Heart Fulfilling the Word
Colossians Chapter-I Verses 24-26

<u>Introduction</u>: The writer is the Apostle Paul from jail in Rome. (Saved on Damascus Rd) 3 missionary trips [collected offering for poor saints @ Judea] arrested @ Jerusalem [taken to Rome for trial [friends gone] like Jesus @ Gethsemane [friends could not watch for 1-hour]. Thought: Preachers & pastors are often alone [even when friends/family are around] they see the outside but never know what he faces inside. [agony, drops of blood, the future] but he must have a servant's heart to endure hardness as a good soldier.

<u>Role</u>: The preacher's role is to always expect God to act. A visitor comes to Rome [Epaphras] pastor of the church @ Colosse. Became a believer @ Ephesus [went out of the way @ Ephesus and again @ Rome]. Preached out the church @ Colosse. But left the flock to save a single one [left the 99] although his leadership was key & he was thought to be a success, he went to see his spiritual father. The evidence in the report talked of stability, growth, and loyalty. But there had crept in a smidgen [morsel, bit] of untruth [like leaven-harm salvation]. In this valley there was a chemical called lycus that aided the growth of wool [results]. A new group with money @ Colosse began to teach Gnosticism [the worship of angels rather than Christ]. Like cancer, this lie began to spread [circumcism, shaved heads, old] and soon would eat away the life of the church. Like colic to a newborn, this untruth would get rid of the pastor if the pastor did not get rid of it.

Epaphras recognized his limitations [pastor with a servant's heart]. Not like the disciples that challenged the evil spirit @ the temple. Now & then problems will creep into Powerhouse [groups, schisms, challenges, I rather than we] and the pastor must seek God's advice. Like Moses [water, bread, meat, judging] when faced with problems, he must seek God. But Epaphras got arrested [Paul's teaching was so good]. So Paul uses 2 men to support the mission and carry the letter back to Colosse [God always has somebody to stand in to help]. The Bible is filled with those that stood in to help. [Aaron & Joshua with Moses][Joshua @ Caleb as spies][4 men that bore the mat for the lame man][Nicodemus & Joseph of Arimathea]. The pastor cannot be everything to every-body. He needs help to fill the simple desires of the church. If he follows God's will, he will make some folk mad. He must consult & abide in God's will. [problem with the Grecian widows just 1-yr after Pentecost-food]. The pastor must concentrate on God's word. The disciples went to town one day while in Samaria; upon their return they saw Jesus talking to a woman [Rabbi's did not].

<u>Relationship</u>: This jailed missionary & proud pastor formed a bond [prisoners together]. They do not see their situation as punishment but service. We [saints]

complain about our situation, but if we saw it as a chance to tell the world about a Savior, we would help the world. We complain about money, spouse, children, choir, ushers, deacons, and church. But down in Philippi, while in jail, Paul & Silas held a prayer meeting that made a change in a jailer's heart. When we suffer for Christ, He rejoices. These men had reached a level of concentration that confirmed the belief that [we may build cathedrals..but only what we do for Christ will last]. In his relationship with Christ, Paul had developed a servant's heart. He joined this walk of salvation so that they could serve the church, not himself. "Eve", the helpmeet [church, the bride, is supposed to be the Lord's help- meet].

This world needs to know about Jesus Christ. [He is not here in the flesh] But his body, the church, is here. We are those that have been called out [separated] sanctified [filled] baptized with the Holy Ghost and with fire. That is the great mystery hidden in Christ by God. Mysteries were ideas and thoughts that made a way out of no way for those that loved Him. [ark-rod-manna-church]. These mysteries brought on a secret society that wanted to produce a false togetherness. Scribes, Pharisees, & Sadducees reserved this mysterious society for themselves [honor in marketplace, endeared them to widows, got them paid during trials, seats @ church, raised their bankbooks]. That is why they questioned Jesus about his authority [whose payroll?].

But God had revealed the mystery of the church to saints in stages. Too much too soon would hurt not help the church [Jesus said.."there are many things I want to tell you now, but you cannot handle it, but when the Holy Spirit comes, he will tell you all things]. In the wilderness just after leaving Egypt [tabernacle], and in Jerusalem just after David desired to build God a house [temple], and then in the world of salvation just after the Holy Ghost fell on the earth [church] for those that have been blessed of the Lord.

The reason I know Gnosticism is a lie is because angels did not die for me [rise from the grave, leaning post, did not forgive me of all my sins, delivered me from all my problems, all issues, all concerns, did not promise never to leave me, are not preparing a place for me, will not come back to receive me unto themselves, so that where they are, I will also be]. I will keep worshipping Jesus [even the angels worship Him].

<u>Responsibility</u>: That is why it is important for the pastor to fulfill the word of God. These man-made mysteries, produced to imitate God consist of un- truths that block the mind of God's liberty.[knights-masons-court/calanthia-fra- ternaties-sororities-secret systems-KKK-brotherhoods-sisters-mafia-gangs]. But the greatest secret society I know is the saints. That society has a power from on high unseen by men that do not know the Master [car with more speed than used, then has a passing gear]. Businesses have loans, collateral, assets. But when debts threaten the business, the government provides a subsidy [subsidizes]. The saint has loans [love] and collateral [saved soul] and assets [gifts]. But when sin

sometimes gets the best of us and threatens our relationship with Christ, we go to God [government] and He gives us more Holy Ghost [subsidizes our weak abilities] and restores us to rightful fellowship.

The pastor has to fulfill the word because he understands the power of the Holy Ghost and knows that it is just enough [family-friends-foes]. One day Peter was accused as a traitor for going down to Cornelius' house. But he was sent there to fulfill the word. [God had said…"one day, I will pour out my spirit upon all flesh"] Peter explained that I saw the need to go in a vision. And when I got there, meat that I thought could not be eaten, was served [rise Peter, slay and eat], then, when I started speaking about Jesus Christ, the Holy Ghost fell on them, and they started speaking in tongues, just like we did on the day of Pentecost] So I know that as a preacher, my job is to fulfill the word.

<u>Closing</u>: Maybe our secret way is seen in how we clap our hands [we pat our feet] shut for joy [praise the Lord]. All of the mysteries hidden for ages have been revealed to saints of God. Many things were hidden in the Old Testament, but now revealed through the New Testament. Altar [Jesus Christ] Mercy-seat [Jesus Christ]; manna [Bread of Life]; candlestick [light of the world]; gates to the city [Jesus, the door]; jubilee [Resurrection]; vineyard [true vine]; steps of a good man [way-truth-life]; scape-goat [lamb of God].

I know, I know, I got work to do. Work as a pastor means [getting orders from up above] but it means putting up with painful things below. I know, I know, I got work to do. Work with a servant's heart means helping others that cannot help themselves. I know, I know, I got work to do. And, I want leave you when I tell you this. One day, a man asked what does it take to be a real good pastor. The answer came back that a man must do 3 things. No-3, he must be willing and able to render service. No-2 he must be holy and live right. But no-1 is he has to have love in his heart. Without love, I am nothing. Though I speak, with the tongues, of men, and angels; and, have not charity, in my heart. I am, sounding brass, and, tinkling cymbals.

Love moves, a many mountain. Love crosses a many sea. Love hides, a many fault. Love covers a many mistake. God is love. For God so loved the world, that He gave His only Son. And, whosoever, believeth in Him, shall not perish, but have [do you want to live forever] I say we can have, everlasting life]

Good evening now children. God bless your hearts. I'm going back to my seat. Yes!!!!!!!

Sermon - The Pastor A Man for Mysteries

Colossians Chapter-1 verses 24-29

As believers, we have been taught to think that all will be OK once we give our lives to the Lord. A few young men with the desire think that pastoring is easy and brings rewards. But here in this passage we want to share with you that stuff may get worse before it gets better. This passage, written by the Apostle Paul to the church @ Colosse finds the man converted on the Damascus Rd. in a Roman jail cell. Having worked to raise an offering for the starving churches in Judea, Paul was arrested @ Jerusalem and sent to Rome. Witnesses create falsehoods to testify so that he would get punished. But the real reason for their lies are so that the gospel of Jesus Christ is stopped before it reaches the whole world. So it seems that just after doing good, this great preacher gets in return something bad. [examples today]. He recalls the promise of the Lord when leaving to return to Heaven; "I will never leave you, neither forsake you, even until the end of the age". But, the evidence is shaky. His spiritual son Timothy has been dispatched to Ephesus. His spiritual son Titus had been left in Crete. His good friend Crescents is gone to Galatians. He needs to send his beloved and trusted companions Tychicus and Onesimus back to Colosse with letters for the Colossians and Ephesians. His former friends Demas and Hermogenes have deserted him. Only Luke is with him. Sometimes the devil will make it seem like everybody has run out on you. But the servant's heart withstands the wiles of the devil.

This theme passage of scripture, written about AD-64 cross-references with the words spoken by Jesus in the book of John just days before his death. In John, the Master gives to us the role, relationship, and responsibility of those that love him unconditionally. In the 12th chapter @ verse-26, He begins with the word if; a word that is infant with the possibility of growing up, and calls for a man to make up his mind about whom he will serve. Joshua had called for the same thing centuries earlier. Serving Christ means obeying Christ. The word follow addresses the need to get behind the Lord and allow Him to lead us. And if we follow Him, naturally we are where He is, and if we are with him, the Father will honor us. Our roles as Christians bring us into the relationship of fellowship with the Godhead and make us responsible for serving mankind for the benefit of Jesus Christ.

Epaphras, the great leader of the church @ Colosse goes to Rome to visit with Paul. [leave church and go to jail to visit a prisoner?] We have a high time @ church but a low time after leaving church. He went to bring Paul a good report about the church [pastors do that]. He tells about the general conditions that seem favorable. The church is growing and yet loyal to Paul. But there is also something troubling. There is growing discontent among the brethren over matters that lay just beneath the surface. Out of eyesight and earshot of the Pastor is the teaching of visiting Jews that in order to be saved, one must trust in the doctrine of angels. This false philosophy called Gnosticism was pregnant with mischief for the infant church. It was like the colic that attacks the breathing system of a newborn. Soon it would snuff out the life of the church and the Pastor knew that if he did not get rid of it. It would soon get rid of the church. [Sin is like an infection]. Like teaching that circumcism is important to salvation, angel worship is a lie that harms the truth. Epaphras is so caught up in the teaching of Paul that he is arrested too. Since he is in jail, there seems to be nobody to carry the letter back to Colosse. But God always has a ram in the bush. To this unlikely scene comes a runaway slave named Onesimus, belonging to a friend named Philemon that meets Paul during a stay in jail and is converted. Onesimus had come to Rome to rid himself of his past and develop for himself a bright future. [church is like Rome]. God uses folk that are former slaves to be mailmen for the gospel. So Paul writes that Jesus Christ is pre-eminent above all things. Above Greek philosophy. Above Egyptian jewels. Above Babylonian beauty. Above Roman Legislation. Above American culture. The sufficiency of Christ is always on trial. Men try to invent other items of interest to refute the notion that Jesus is all you need. But His is the name above every name. It is at His name that every knee shall bow and every tongue shall confess.

But reading the letter we notice that the 1st chapter is piled high with this pastors fervent love. In vs. 1-8 Paul offers praise for the church. In vs. 9-14 Paul offers prayer for the church. In verses 24-29 Paul extends a proclamation to the church.

In verse 24, Paul begins with the word who [Christ] rejoices with me in my sufferings for your benefit. The pastor suffers for the benefit of the church. Right now, while in prison, in chains, in darkness, in pain, Paul yet rejoices. [do we rejoice in the bad times?] And, Paul says he is filling up that body of believers called out of darkness because of the afflictions of Christ. Here is a slave with a servant's heart working to advance the church. With his flesh, Paul focuses on the death, the burial, and the resurrection of Jesus. His views are firm on the cross, the tomb, the sacrifice, and the blood. He wants to talk about nothing else but the nails, the sponge, the final words from that cross. For his body [call-out], the interests of the church demanded he endure the afflictions of mankind as a good soldier [his Master did]. This gospel for gentiles and the existence of the church were bound together. Christ loved the church and gave himself for it.

But there was a secret system of false beliefs that exercised vast influence over the minds of scholars and learned men, even in Christ's day. Even the Jewish church @ Alexandria wanted to expand Judaism through symbols, crests, and numerical substitutes that would veil the inner doctrines from the eyes and ears of believers. [gangs & graffiti]. All this stuff had been hidden. Unknown to those that carried on in the name of the Lord. Men had challenged Jesus to produce certain credentials every time He worked a miracle. [Scribes, Pharisees, &

Sadducees reserved miracles for themselves]. That is what preserved for them seats of honor in the congregation. It endeared them to widows. It tightened their relationships with Rome. It fixed their bank accounts with publicans. It strengthened their holds on the rules makers and helped guide verdicts when trails were held.

But now that Christ has died and been raised from the dead, all mystical events in the unseen world are exposed to the saints of God. The use of the words made manifest in verse 26 points to a divine act that was forced to occur to indicate that God, in Christ Jesus, challenged the unseen world to hide needed elements called for the survival of the church. His resurrection was unseen. And he did it to show the world that unseen does not mean untrue. Death was a secret society for satanic followers. They used blood in their rituals. The cross was used to keep back those that were called vampires. Nails were used for the symbols of flakes being held together under pressure. Only those that were involved in this secret society of the underworld knew to use these symbols to defeat the weak.

Paul knew about this stuff. His private-school education @ the feet of the most learned men in Jerusalem afforded him the privilege of awareness of these tricks. The Pastor must be aware of these tricks today. Prosperity is not a sufficient salve for the sore of sin. The preacher must have private schooling from God himself to be able to ward off tricks of the devil.

In verse 25, Paul says that I became a minister. I did not start out as one but I am a member now. As the church's minister, Paul was bound to toil and accept afflictions in every way the church and its' welfare required. Paul knew about house management and understood its' arrangement regarding stewardship. As the chief steward over God's house, Paul was to be the confidential "upper-servant" that is totally responsible to the Master. [story of Joseph]. From this position, Paul dispenses and distributes the gospel. He uses the term dispensation to obligate the firm truth of all mysteries that had been hidden by and in God. [Ark, Rod, manna, Church] Allowed to see it and to serve it. These truths were given to Paul because God knew he would not mishandle it. Too many men selected as pastors do not have a heart for the people. God has an eye for those that will work to fulfill the word of God. He knows what ingredients to add that will complete the task and give full development to the church. To further the mysteries hidden in Him, we see the family structure expand to the tabernacle when Israel left Egypt. We see God expand the tabernacle from a tent to a temple when David wants God to have a house. We see God expand the temple to the church as the ecclesiastical body borne for the purpose of unfolding doctrinal truths that, although hidden for ages, are brought to the light for the good of those that love the Lord and are called according to his purposes.

When you see the word mysteries in scripture, Paul is challenging the system of secret initiations granted to select few and made known only to those allowed into that special society. [Masons, knights, court of Calanthia, fraternities, sororities, KKK, brotherhoods, sisterhoods, Mafia, leadership teams].

But God took those symbols of death, blood, nails, and the cross and created a secret society called salvation. And only those that have been given the secret handshake, called the right hand of fellowship, can be admitted. Only those that have been granted citizenship in this invisible kingdom through an oath of obedience shall be permitted to fight under the bloodstained banner of Christ. Only those that have been washed in the blood of the crucified lamb shall be allowed to stand behind the great white throne of judgment. To those gave he the right to move from children of men to be called sons & daughters of Christ. The Apostle Peter had discovered this secret society. The disciples were aware of it too. That is why they argued about positions of power to be held in the kingdom that was unseen by men.

But on the day of Pentecost, the Holy Ghost fell on those men and after that they received power that introduced them to this secret society. When the Jews for going down to Cornelius' house challenged Peter, Peter wanted to acquit their blame. The folk questioned his association with this captain of the Roman guard. So Peter told his accusers that he remembered the words of the haggard prophet, John the Baptist. John told them that I baptize you with water. But one comes after me, whose shoelaces I am unworthy to latch, He shall baptize you with the Holy Ghost and fire. Peter did not know what that meant then, but when he got to Cornelius' house, and began to speak about Jesus, the Holy Ghost fell on Cornelius' house just like it fell on the Jewish believers on the day of Pentecost; and they began to speak with other tongues. Confirming too, that they had been saved.

So if this secret society has a set of silent symbols, it must be the way we clap our hands. It must be the way we pat our feet. It must be the way we shout to express our joy. And if this secret society has a silent language unknown by the those that are unsaved, it must be the way we utter strange words of praise, our cries, or the way we wave our hands, and the tongues we speak to express our relationship with God.

In verse 27, Paul writes that it is the saints to whom God would make known this great mystery. He used a Greek term in the original text that outlines God's will. It was God's will that these revelations are so momentous in occurrences, so outstanding in the method, so different from human foresight, not swayed by the prejudices on men, that it had to be from God himself. Peter said that when God began to speak Hebrew to me through the mouth of Cornelius, "who was I to withstand God?" [church-today]. Because the riches of God's glory are the graces he uses to make transformations of sin-sick souls to recipients of royal righteousness brought on by the grace of God given to those that do not deserve His favor. Where are those riches right now? They are in you. Christ in you, the hope of glory.

This hope that your pastor tells you about, can be seen when you love your enemy. This hope that he lifts off the page of scripture and places on your spiritual plates Sunday after Sunday can be felt when we treat our neighbors as ourselves. This hope that he keeps before your eyes can make you pray for those that despitefully use you. This hope is seen when you go the 2nd mile. This hope is joyously embraced when you give up your coat to a freezing friend. This hope is shared when you can turn the other cheek for the purpose of being slapped again. So that when others ask you how you do it, you can say "it ain't me that you see, but the Christ that is within me".

My brothers and sisters, Heaven ought not just be your destination. Heaven ought to be your motivation. Because Heaven is where we will wear different attire. You know how it is when our wives know their class reunions are coming up. They buy a new dress that often is too tight to fit on the day they buy it. But they are motivated to lose a few pounds so that by the time the event comes, the dress is going to fit just right. Well, that's the way we ought to be motivated for Heaven. If our feet are to wear golden slippers, we ought not want them to stand in the way of sinners. If our heads are destined to wear a golden crown, then we ought not let our heads be filled with anger, envy, and hate. If our bodies are to be borne by the wings of angels, then, we ought to be ready to mortify these old bodies so that we can be found without spot, wrinkle, or blemish. You see, the rights of the believer are complete in Christ. The sinner can be forgiven by accepting Him today as Lord and Savior.

In verse 28, Paul paints his portrait further as a herald of the good news of Jesus Christ. But he shows his unselfishness by using the word "we". Look at the word Powerhouse. I see the word we, but not the word I. Your pastor is unselfish. That is the mark of the servant. Unselfish. Paul had been sitting in his jail cell listening to Epaphras talk about those that belonged to his church @ Colosse. But at the same time this pastor talked about others, he was telling Paul something about himself. You might not believe me but you tell your pastor a lot about yourself when you talk about somebody else. Epaphras did not come to Rome to help himself. He came to Rome to help his church. Your pastor did not take this position to help just him. He was called by God to help you. He is interested in finding ways to <u>warn every man</u>. Little did he know at the time that he was warning men today with his letter. The pastor must be prepared to <u>teach all men</u>. And Paul tells those @ Colosse that their pastor has the zeal for them and is working fervently in prayer, that he might find a way to <u>teach them in all wisdom</u>. His real aim is to <u>present them as perfect in Christ Jesus.</u> Here the Apostle used a term that means "fully-grown". We are born again as children [babes in Christ]. When we argue and get mad at the least little things, our infancy is showing. When we cry for attention, refuse to serve because our name is not on program, stop coming because somebody made us mad, we are just showing our spiritual age. But when we stand in front of our families and face our persecutors, then we have matured and are prepared to be perfect. [Abraham when another man looked @ Sarah; when he went to save Lot].

In verse 29, the pastor with a servant's heart is always working & striving to grow the saint. He gets weary but does not wear out. He gives out but never gives up. Sometimes his emotions get the best of him. But he is encouraged by the words of his Master in the Garden of Gethsemane, "not my will but thine be done". The pastor recognizes that opponents will contend for the faith of the flock. Folk will accuse him of many things. The flock will complain about water and yet complain of its' bitterness when found. The flock will complain about their lack of meat; then complain when the meat gets stuck in their teeth. But the pastor knows that this toil must be sustained because leadeth beside still water.

Oh, he understands that "we wrestle not against flesh and blood, but against principalities, against powers, against the rulers of the darkness of this world, against spiritual wickedness in high places". That is why we must put on the whole armour of God, that we might be able to withstand in the evil day, and having done all to stand. We can stand with our lions girt about with truth, having the breastplate of righteousness; feet shod with the preparation of the gospel of peace; the shield of faith; the helmet of salvation; and the sword of the spirit, which is the word of God". We can quench the fiery darts of the wicked.

So as I leave you today with verse 29, where Paul says that the energy of his Master is divine in concept, strong in ability, unbelievable to sight, special in duty, joyous in hope, radiant in appearance, and confident in love. And that power is still working in the pastor. The pastor opens this mystery to God's called out saints. He reveals Christ as the open secret of the Old Testament and presents these understandings.
Altar [Christ]; Mercy-seat [Christ]; Manna [Bread of Life]; Water [wells of living water] Candlestick [Light of the world]; Gate [the Door]; Shepherd [good Shepherd]; Jubilee [Resurrection]; Vineyard [true Vine]; Steps of a good man [Way-Truth-Life]; Scape-goat [Lamb of God].
Good evening now children, I am going back to my seat. But one day, a man asked what it takes to be a good pastor. The answer comes back that no-3, he has to be ready to render service. No-2, he has to be holy and live right. But no-1 is that he has to love. Without love, though I speak with the tongues of men and angel, and have not charity..[sounding brass & tinkling cymbals].

Sermon – Indications of Infancy
I Corinthians Chapter-2 verse 16 thru Chapter-3 verse 4

Introduction: One of the things we as Christians need to work at but seldom think about is whether or not we are really growing as believers. If most died like we are today, few of us would actually go to Heaven. Most of us think it is the others that go to Church with us that need improvement. But not us. This letter from Paul is one that we can view this afternoon as a warning to us. When he visited Corinth, he found a collection of believers that still warred among themselves; even after conversion. He received the news that they were yet troubled by partisanship. Choosing sides. We see indications of infancy when Christianity is not the dominant force [little faith with lots of flesh]. He found folk hindered by Satan at every turn. Infants show themselves by staying on the edge [truth love, faith, care, trust, and belief]. Illustration of tribe-Gad and gadderenes. Infants are of no credit to Christ. Infants make Christianity questionable to the world around them. Paul says in vs.-16, that it takes the mind of the Master for a person to receive instructions from the Lord. Our spirit is so weak, disconnected; we cannot believe the promises of God. So Paul paints a picture for us with the hope we can see ourselves. Are we babes? Are we adults. Let's look.

Every true believer knows that we must be born again. That indicates we enter this walk as babes. But you might recall that the theory of the new birth was a problem to understand even for the Gynecologist, Nicodemus. Jesus had to step his teaching down to a primary level and use the wind to show the prominent doctor truths about Heaven. God's plan is birth, growth, and maturity. Paul's says that our Lord seeks a change in man so that man can change the world. He seeks fruit, more fruit, and much fruit. What he receives is faults, more faults, and many faults. Look at physical life. [1ˢᵗ natural and then spiritual]. In children, we treat them with vitamins/minerals to speed up their growth. We give them the utmost care and take them to the doctor for periodic checkups. But we neglect to take spiritual vitamins and minerals [bible study and praying/fasting]. We require checkups every Sunday [neglect to attend church]. Some people in this world grow old but never grow up. [Christian world too]. The passage we study today indicates that same problem. [never grew up].

<u>First, the spiritual infant is disturbed with self</u>. [do not look for change]. The word carnal is a combination of cardiac and natural. Creation rather than the Creator dominates converts with earthly hearts. [world but not worship]. Positively, they should recognize their dependence and trust their provider. But negatively, they as babes crave for attention. They are of no practical use @ church. They cannot be relied upon for attendance [late]. They draw upon the resources of the church. Hold an exalted opinion of self/family/actions. Anxious for accolades and acknowledgement. Instable, fretful, peevish [love small things] never satisfied w/anything, often depressed, faultfinders. You will also

see a fondness for toys. They embrace ornate rituals, pretty pictures, gaudy decorations, and every celebration [weddings, funerals, baptisms, banquets, cantata, contest]. They are not open minded [know a little but think they know it all]. A carnal Christian seldom finds peace and feels better when they are @ war. The bible tells us about the disciples that argued over the top spots.

So Paul came to this church and found a wounded organism. Hurting because they fought among themselves. He worries about their diet. [milk rather than meat] He worries about their dress [diapers rather than robes]. He worried about their duties [talk rather than work]. Infants get upset over the smallest things. They are impatient and unteachable. I tried to tell you the truth about the cross, but you would hear nothing about it. Paul says you were not able to bear it then and even now; you don't want to hear it. [Importance of the cross in salvation]. Paul found a church filled with folk that he had to handle with kid gloves. They were like time bombs..always close to exploding. [nice @ church; nasty @ home] [ideal @ church; impossible @ home][praising @ home; pouting @ church] [grouch @ home; good @ church]. Most infants are all talk. Do all kind of stuff to be seen. [programs, out front, teachers, play music, ushers, etc]. Infants are receivers not givers [tithes, encouragement, humility]. They examine everything. If I ask you to point out the infants, whom would you point to?

<u>Secondly, the infant is dedicated to argument</u>. No matter what you say, they will reply..yes, but. Paul indicates in his letter that they are still filled with envy, strife, and divisions. Envy, the trouble most face when we decide to not outdo another. Jealousy raged among the Corinthians and stunted their growth. This thing called envy generates rivalries and sets folk against one another so much so that they become recruiters to form gangs in the church to help fight those that they hate. God might love them but not the infant. Then there is strife. Perhaps the most underestimated sin in our lives is strife. In Galatians, Paul says that strife results from manifestations of the flesh. In Philippians Paul says, "let nothing be done through strife and vainglory". In Colossians Paul says, "forebear with one another and forgive one another as Christ has forgiven you". In 1 Thessalonians Paul says "and the Lord make you to increase and abound in love one toward another". So the idea of a Christian is to put up with one another. There was great diversity among the disciples. Between them we find entrepreneurs, an IRS agent, secret informers, traitors, doubters. They never fought, but they wanted to fight. Have you ever watched children fight? Unfair is how they fight. Never wanting adults to solve the problem. Just join my side. Infants never want to share unless they get the bigger share. Then there are divisions in the church. Diversity is found in God's law, gifts, insight, creation [153 species of fish]. Christianity was made up of Jews, Romans, and Greeks. There were differences when they arrived but there was to be a homogenization of providence after they came. Did you know that division is the residue of bitterness and that bitterness aggravates animosities and causes serious health issues for people [even Christians]? This is the result of staying an infant too long. [midgets and children]. Some have said that churches are but organizations with the same

opinion about Jesus. Class conscience [rich/poor][educated/uneducated][old/young][sick/well]. Infants??

<u>Thirdly, spiritual infants dependent on people rather than Christ</u>. The church @ Corinth was split over which preacher had made the biggest impact. They became followers of the person under whim they were converted. But we need to avoid that malady. At birth, we meet the OB-Gyn. During our youth, we meet a pediatrician. During our formative years, we meet a primary care physician. During our old age, we meet a geriatric. That means one doctor does not serve our growth needs throughout life. So, in like manner, one preacher may not be able to provide all spiritual growth for the believer throughout his spiritual life. But the words "I am of Paul" indicates that person thought he/se only had to listen to Paul. [a result of that theory leads to disaster]. An infant's world is made up of family/familiarity/routines. Church folk can be like too. [no change, no raise, no tolerance]. If mother does not come when crying, they scream [tantrums]. Spiritual infants look to human resources to solve their greatest needs.

Closing: But what shall we do with those of us that remain childlike? Some would ask they be dismissed. But children that are thrown out of the house seldom grow up on their own. Although Jesus did not teach the cross early; they needed to hear it taught. He waited but He taught them about the cross. They like us preferred human-divine; personal-universal; selfish-spiritual; and the temporary-permanent. We must know that some preachers are good for some flocks but terrible for others. Paul condemned even those that were selecting his doctrine only. For he said that each preacher provided some part of the crops assistance. But that God would water and grow the crop. As adults, we stop allowing human passion to dictate and dominate our thoughts and actions. Look to Christ as the author and finisher. Hold fast to the short time left in this life with the idea that soon [and very soon] we shall stand before Him [either in trembling fear or the hope of glory. Some folk drive a long ways to attend a movie, see a game, support some organization, hear a preacher, listen to a choir, sing, and go to a program. They pay large sums to attend. Even save for days so they can pay. But they cannot afford to tithe on Sunday. They cannot afford to support their pastor with a call [he should call me]. They cannot attend church on time [late]. They cannot participate in any program [too tired]. They will not reach out to connect with another to build up Christ so that God gets the glory [infants]. And the signs are everywhere.

Story of the little boy at home on Saturday night. Conversation he heard went like this. The phone was the office [not home]. The check at the eatery was too low [their tough luck]. The radar detector worked [saved tickets]. The hot refrigerator kept things cool [bargain]. Later as the boy finished his lesson for Sunday School [happy dad was no longer mad [cheating on his test].

Sermon – Being Down On Your Luck
St. Luke   Chapter-20: 45 to Chapter 21:4

<u>Introduction</u>: Every day, it seems that the newspapers bring us news that is worse than the day before. Our economic woes have reached a level where the report is that more folk are in poverty than in recent memory. And, we all know that when folk cannot eat or feed themselves that wars and crime rise. All of that trouble is basically caused by the sins of mankind. Some are caused by neglect. Others by mistakes. Still, most are caused by greed. But I want you to see that our Lord was concerned about how well people do, even in a spiritual sense, He is worried how we handle pressure; especially when we are down on our luck.

Think with me, of friends, family, and even foes that may be struggling right now. Jobs [lost], income [strained], bank accounts [dropping], help [nowhere to be found]. Loans [no], advance [uh-uh], and credit [abuse on the rise]. So, we come to the text to tell us what another person did when down on her luck and perhaps what we should do when we are down on ours.

<u>Background</u>: All of chapter 20 deals with finances. The scribes question the support Jesus has to address issues of normal life as He does. [Who pays you to do this? Motives?] They inquire about ownership [vineyard], income taxes [render], they offer up recycling [resurrection]. Then He questions them about trust. And that's a good question for us today. Who do we trust? Before they can answer, He gives them advice starting in verse-45. Right in front of everybody. He says watch out for *frauds to the faith*. Preachers that tell you what you want to hear so you will feel better, rather than tell you the truth so that you will act better [be better] [live better]. He goes on to identify signs of a fraudulent religion [today]. They dress to be seen (today) [long robes hard to walk in]. They love to hear their names called [today-greetings in the market]. They prefer to be greeted by ushers and shown to their favorite seats [today highest seats @ synagogue]. They enter late and want to be served early [today-chief rooms @ feasts]. That ain't all. Josephus, the great historian, tells us that these folk held their religious leaders in high esteem. <u>*High maintenance*</u>. The widows went to them for advice about investments. Widows [indeed] w/o protection, producer, provider, promoter, went to ask about securing their inheritance for their futures. These leaders were members of the town council {Sanhedrin} and knew of legislative transactions, foreclosures, forfeitures, and failures, and were to steer the widows to risk-free investments. But chose to guide them in ways where the widows' money would end up in the leaders' pockets. That is what He means by devouring widows houses [eating up the widows retirement]. They practiced their prayers. But would be condemned before it is all over. Jesus would have us know that things can change rather quickly. Mine today [problems]. Yours tomorrow. [Job] [David] [Noah] 3-Hebrew boys] [Daniel] Some here today.

Here Christ introduces us to a certain widow. He has already been teaching at Church, and the text tells us that she has been listening too. Men could go into the Temple, but women were restricted to the outer court. So she had leaned, listened, and learned great truths about the faith of folk when funds are low. It is not hard to be faithful when everything is going well. But it is so difficult to believe when things are a struggle. Our minds whisper lies, quote falsehoods, makes us question everybody, we trust nobody. Not even God. [Name, age, appearance, children-none, address, sick/well]. But what we do know is that she had little funds; but a lot of faith. The text tells us what to do when we are down on our luck.

First, it tells us where we ought to go. She went to church. Broke folk often develop excuses [clothes, tired, rich, ashamed, no money]. But our usefulness is of greater benefit.

Secondly, what we ought to do is be compelled to give. To give us a contrast, Jesus sees the rich putting in their gifts. 13 horn-like pots along the wall on your way out were places to insert your gifts. These men are not down on their luck. But He sees our giving. Everything we give, He sees. Giving affects your character as well as your circumstances. Giving is an action that is the difference between international good and incidental evil. Giving is a permanent influence and reproductive as well. Giving is a seed in the soil that spouts and feeds many in the days ahead. Two pennies. Not much by earthly accounting. But more than any of us have ever given by Heaven's accounting. What do we give, when down on our luck? [What do we give when we are not down on our luck?] If at heart we are selfish, then in the judgment of God our gifts are without virtue. (1) The gift of money; The widow's mite was more than the gold of the rich. Why? Because they gave in their abundance [no pain, they would not miss it] and she gave all she had. (2) The gift of time; The man whose circumstances allow him to contribute much time and talent to the cause of religion and philanthropy may be making a small contribution. In comparison to that man that toils all week and yet shows to mow and paint and clean. The rich can afford to hire. But the poor can afford to come. (3) Active service; this is the service of Christian labor. Some study to teach, while others do nothing but come to be taught [complain, find fault, block progress, tare it up]. (4) The sacrifice of life; Folk today would think that all that died for the cause have given the same gift for God. But not so my friends. Life has very different values when taken at different stages. It is comparatively little for a man that has spent his days doing as he pleases and yet when he is old comes to do the Lord's will. [explain the importance of all but press the need to come early]. Solomon said "remember they Creator in the days of thy youth! Think how tough it is for he that has all of life ahead [pleasures, discoveries, prizes] yet he dedicates his life to Christ. [3-Hebrew boys, Joseph, David].

But the third thing we ought to do when down on our luck is seek ways to give

<u>more than before</u>. Job gave all he had before getting twice as much. Since our Master sees all that we do, He sees her gift as the largest gift of the day. He told His disciples that she gave more than the rest. Although they had cheated her, she did not point them out nor try to stifle the Church. God measures our gifts by our ability to give. Too often, we point out what others did with their money [cars, houses, clothes, jewelry, vacation, big-time, children]. Imagine the inward struggle about this gift. What would you do if the request was for your last? Although she would leave the Church with nothing in her pocket, she left with much joy in her heart. She had come to the Temple unknown [today] but she left with a greater reputation than any that attended that day [today]. The gift of faith is measured not by what we give, but by what we keep. Let us take care that we do not judge by the appearance only. We do not know the situation of another's life or hardships. Let us also be sure that every act of kindness is true, worthy, and appreciated.

Conclusion: What if we had been living during that special day. What would we have said about the widow if we had observed her offering? Stingy? Selfish? New suit but old tricks? Had we known her for a while, would we have added up her purchases and decided she spent poorly and now.."it serves her right". Is this the attitude we want others to have about us? Many of us have not shown faith in our tithing. We give only when we have everything else covered. But I need to warn us today that the Bible says lay up your gifts for God the first day not the last day. Before you pay the light man, the gas man, the milk man. Before you pay the car note, the house note, the clothes note. For God is the great giver of every good and perfect gift. He is the great giver of all things new. He is the giver because He gave His only Son; and the Son gave His life. God gives eternal life to all that believe in His Son.
The message on a tombstone in England says;

- What I spent, I had
- What I saved, I lost
- What I gave, I gained

Sermon – The Valley of Trouble
Hosea; Chapter-2; vss. 14-17

<u>Introduction</u>: This passage is about a period of Israel's history when they were exceedingly difficult to govern. God has, it seems, exhausted His earthly attempts at corrections, and now resorts to using unnatural approaches to show them to themselves. Wrong yet right. Bad yet good. Wayward yet worshippers. Bound for Hell yet for Heaven

This prophet (Hosea) is sought by God to be spokesman to Israel. But his reluctance is found basically in the lack of passion he has to render service. Hosea does not understand why God is vexed with Israel. So God permits him to marry a prostitute, treat her well, give her all she wants, and still she leaves him for another. This woman is styled as Israel [betrothed to God yet desirous of another] the Church [bride of Christ]. But God will through His wonderful ways, purify us so that we will come forth without spot, wrinkle, blemish; filled with hope and ready to serve our husband. [obey].

Israel [wife] has backslidden and gone after Baal [an idol god]. She believes he can make her happier [lies of Satan]. Today, the church is filled with folk just like Gomer. People are seeking money/possessions/ power/reputations and that leads to envy/control freaks. We worship creature comforts/cars/cottages @ country/clubs/careers/choirs. We seek to dominate scenes like music/ mystical/misery/mistakes. These trails lead to mans troubles; because each is a divinely locked door to prohibit passage. But we suffer from "green grass syndrome" [Judas][Rich, young, ruler][Ahab & Jezebel]. You and I suffer too!

But even when we go astray from God, He still loves us and wants us to return. So often, He sends us towards Heaven through the valley of trouble. Walk with me around this text

I. **Relief**: The first thing God does is find a way to give us relief. The scripture text says I will, meaning God himself intervenes. Although we sin, [1*] He longs for us*. [allure]. She deserves desertion but He gives grace. God alters our opinion about gains and moves us to godliness. He slows our trust in temporary things and helps us to trust in eternal things. [2] *He leads us*. The text says He brings her. If we just follow the Lord we cannot go wrong. [3*] He understands us*. The text says He brings us to the place that will do us the most good [wilderness]. We want to be in the penthouse [outhouse]. But Israel listened to God in the wilderness. Egyptian bondage had prepared Israel for liberty. She took instruction in the wilderness [10 commandments]. [4*] He talks with us*. The text says He will speak to her. He wants to comfort us. We are troubled [on every side]. Man speaks to the ear; but God speaks to the heart. His words bring us relief.

II. Redemption: If we are honest, we are failures by ourselves. But He redeems us from destruction. He gives us another chance and all we need do is change.

[1] *He takes chances with us*. The text says He will give us vineyards. We messed up those we were given earlier; but He gives us more chances. [Peter]. Israel had begun to distrust @ Jericho, but God gave them vineyards. Israel had begun to doubt @ Kadesh-Burnea; but God gave them vineyards to help their hope. [when it seems all hope is gone]. [2] *He works miracles to change us*. The text says He transforms obstacles into opportunities. God speaks about the valley of Achor and tells that it will become door of hope. [valley of Achor – place where Achan sinned –tell history]. But God says it will be a source of comfort; hope; joy; rest; peace. The woman that comes back [after repentance] will sing [gladness in heart] as she did when young [delivered] strong voice of Marian @ Red Sea.

III. Restoration: God is looking forward to that time when we are restored to that relationship He had with Adam. [1] *God recognizes that time will restore our respect for Him*. The text says on that day we will call Him our husband. After much trouble, we will return to the love relationship we had before. God uses humbling providence; painful convictions; and distressing circumstances to restore us. [2] *God also sees that we will view Him differently*. We often see Him as a Master. Demanding we serve Him. Thinking horrible thoughts about His voice; call; conquest; challenge. We see Him as an Overseer rather than someone that sees over [hinderer rather than helper][blocker rather than blesser][bad/good] [punisher/promoter][wants you dead/someone that died for you].

IV. Responsive: Finally, God wants us to be responsive. He knows we talk too much; but He worries that we call another name too often. [1] *We trust false gods too often*. The text says God will take away the names of Baalim. These false gods come in all sizes, shapes, and colors. They fall in several categories [lovers – that are idolized friends that become foes and disappoint because they heard a lie about you] [adored children – but life tares them from our embrace][wealth –hoarded, but stripped because our health turns from bad to worse][politics – diplomatic defeats][stock markets – commercial depressions][strength of the army – military disasters like Vietnam]. You see we are folk that love pleasure and wealth; but the Bible says that God will "hedge up thy way with invisible thorns". We need to be purified from immorality, extravagance and self-indulgence. [2] *Lastly, God will give us spiritual alzheimers*. The text says we will remember their names no more. God can make a memory so painful that we will not want to remember the event. God is all-powerful. He uses wind to float one boat and drive another to the rocks. He can use water to quench thirst and yet drown a man with half as much. His way/mind/thoughts.

Closing: God knows how to help us escape from this valley of trouble. Like Israel at Jericho, He has advice that wins every time. Achan was a troubler of Israel; sin is a troubler of mans soul. Achan was to be slain and forsaken [sin], before Israel was to be free to fight and to win. God wants a sorrowful heart; weeping and bitterness because of our sin, repentance. We fancy trouble past, and flatter ourselves into thinking we are better than we are [children, families, bank accounts, cars, houses, looks] But we are faces that shine in the dark. But with God as our witness, His light shines out of darkness [not into darkness]. Joseph [prison] Daniel [lions den] David [persecutions] Christ [cross] we need to know that trouble worketh patience [duty] but our privilege is to rejoice [don't wait until the battle is over]. For our God is able to [bring water from a rock] and He is able [bring salvation to the world through the cross] and then, He is able [to use death as the entrance to eternal life].

One day He opened the door of hope from the valley of trouble [1. world by Christ @ Calvary] and [2. Jew by Joshua @ Achor by slaying Achan and his family] and [3. Sinners by the blood of Jesus in whom we must trust]. Story of Man washing son's hair.

Sermon – Responsible; Respectable; and Resentful

John V; vss. 39-47

<u>Introduction</u>: During this trip to Jerusalem, our Lord has an occasion to manifest His power before those that needed Him most. We must marvel that He demonstrates an ability to heal one that has been sick so long, yet is criticized by those responsible because He did so on the Sabbath. As the respectable Jews rail Him for His work, the Master sees their terrible need. And is amused about the approach they take to make their point. Their anger increases and because of resentment they set out to kill Him because [1] He did what they could not or would not do and [2] His abilities elevated Him above them. Yes, they accused Him of outing Himself equal to God, but they really were mad that He outdid them. [remind the church of today's church folk]. Jesus listens to their talk and recognizes the truth lay at the heart of their search for eternal life. The man @ the pool had been there for 38 yrs. And although the Master had changed his physical condition, the people wondered if his eternal destination had been altered as well. So He sums it up for them in verse 24 "Verily, verily, I say unto you, he that hears my word, and believeth on him that sent me, hath everlasting life, and shall not come into condemnation; but is passed from death to life".

They did not like that. They wanted Him dead. Resentment say no matter of money would suffice. They were now willing to pay it. They did not care with whom they had to make friends. They worried not about whom they had to use, manipulate, take advantage of, lie on, cheat, or ruin. Jesus had to go. (!). But our Lord yet tried to explain the desperate intent of this life. We need to live this life so we can live again. They wanted to do that. But had been blinded by their selfishness and lust for position that they could not see the end for the present [us today]. God has placed in the heart of man a desire to have eternal life. The soul of man yearns for that place where it can rest from labor but also reap a reward that pays for as long as man can enjoy it.

In Jerusalem, there was a ritual of *legalities* that calls attention to us in this case. Men determined to be guilty of crimes and deserving of punishment were sentenced to death and denied choices in life. In Heaven, there is the idea of *spiritualities* that calls attention to us in this case. God determined man guilty of sin and deserving of punishment and sentences that remove us from His wonderful presence. In hell, there is the thought of *eternalities* that calls attention to a final condemnation worthy of wrath and pain that will be endured by those that reject salvation. It is here that the text begins to unfold. [walk with me].

<u>A Commendable Search</u>: Jesus notes here that they were responsible and have been searching for the proper object [eternal life]. [1]. this is man's greatest need

[not money, power, fame, physique, dress] (2) This is man's highest goal. [nothing higher can be given, obtained, achieved] (3) this is man's greatest desire. [Job (diseased, deserted, disappointed, destitute, determined) asked "if a man die, will he live again?] Not only was it a search for the proper object but also in the proper and respectful field. The Scriptures. (4) eternal life is the topic of revelation; natural & essential, and beyond human discovery. [eye has not seen nor ears heard]. And yet they viewed it without merit. The Bible is the only place to be advised about Heaven [wall, streets, trees, water, gates, sickness, sadness, sorrow, people, activities] but He warns them that their hope has lead them into error. For the [b] clause of the 39th vs. says, "for in them ye think ye have eternal life". Search [effort, concerned, diligence] but ye think [their thoughts not His, their minds not His, their opinions not His] Fooled by their own hearts; they became resentful [us today].

A Consequence That's Sad: Most of us have failed to recognize Christ as the great theme of all Scriptures. So their mistake is the same as ours. They would not come to Him and receive life. If we review the state of man's death because of sin, we see he is dead really 3 ways. (1) First he is dead legally. Like a prisoner sentenced to death, his privileges are revoked. God warned Adam "in the day that thou eateth thereof, thou shall surely die". Adam may not have died physically that day, but he died legally. Prisoner [vote, adopt, property, will, bequeath] legally dead. (2) Secondly, he is dead spiritually. Instead of listening to and for God, he begins to make selections on his own [imagination fails-Adam make clothes, morally-hid himself, developed shame, mind is corrupted-practiced lying, integrity shattered-placed blame]. He is dead spiritually in trespasses and sin (3) Thirdly, he is dead eternally. The prisoner is executed finally because he is condemned to death. He is dead eternally because he is dead legally. He is dead eternally because he is dead spiritually. [Cleopatra, Alexander, Sampson, Solomon, David, Lincoln]. Regardless how good each was, they died because of their bad. Rejecting salvation [temporary]

A Cause for Sorrow: Jesus had just declared that the Jews will not come to Him, and now he reveals its cause. Unbelief. "I know that ye have not the love of God in you". This love would have obligated them to seek honor only from God and thus appreciate the glory the Father had given the son. [God's choice] Jesus has no concern for man's praise or report. The Fathers' testimony is all sufficient. "I receive not honor from men". The Jews could not receive this testimony because human considerations had blinded their eyes. "How can you ye believe, when you receive honor from one another". But it went further "and seek not honor that comes from God". He showed them their readiness to receive false Messiahs. "If another comes in his own name, him ye will receive". [church today]. 64 false persons had come to claim themselves as Lord.

A Classic for the Season: They were worried that Jesus was going to accuse them. But Jesus is to be the Judge [not prosecutor]. "Do not suppose that I will accuse you". [thinking wrong]. But Moses their liberator, advocate, redeemer became their accuser. [friend/foe] [helper/hurter]. The Master moved on to show a connection between faith in Jesus and faith in Moses. "For had you believed Moses, ye would have believed me, for he wrote of me". [human instruments]. Christ implies that Moses was the writer of the first 5 books. {Genesis-head bruiser]. Jesus here implies that the whole system of symbols speaks about Him [manna, ark, cloud, candlestick, oil, fire, blood on the door, smoke]. Disbelief in Moses carried with it a disbelief in Christ. "if ye believed not his words, how shall ye believe my words". Now and then we trust things written in a book. [constitution; education; proclamations] and then things that stand the test of time [prestige of age; usage].

<u>Closing</u>: Many that read the Bible are scripturally rich but spiritually poor. Bountiful in the head but bankrupt in the heart. They love to talk about folk but cannot stand talking to folk. They see life as a one-way street. All income but no outcome. Morally, they do nothing. But when gossip comes to call, they do it all. If these men could have healed and helped that cripple at the pool, they would have gotten honor from the crowd. But because Jesus did it himself, they set out to rid the town of the troublemaker. Many today reject Jesus [rules; standards; commitments; obedience; trust; believe; love; but not just Him; love neighbors as self; pray; help]. Sin had made a slave of the Jews. They avoided calling God's name and believed they honored Him. But they were not willing to help one another and that dishonored Him.

Story about Leonard Holt. Responsible for lab work @ the paper mill for 19 years. Respectable in his community [husband, father, boy scout leader, volunteer fireman, deacon, admired by one and all]. A great huntsman with a marksman eye, he caused bloodshed one October evening with 5 guns and just 13 minutes. He killed 15 men and wounded 23 more. Finally, he took his own life. The investigation revealed that Holt had been passed over 12 times by 3 supervisors. So he shot killed all 15 men. Men in the carpool quit riding with him because he began driving so recklessly. This man was brimming with resentment. Rage that could no longer be held in check. In the story found in Time Magazine, beneath the article on Leonard Holt were the words responsible, respectable, and resentful.

You know, it's like that in the church.

Sermon – Why Our Present Hope Should Be in God

James; Chapter-IV; vs. 13-17

<u>Introduction</u>: James [brother of Jesus] was born and raised in same home @ Nazareth; represents the great sin of blindness nest to Jesus but did not know Jesus]; relocated to Capernaum [when Jesus started his earthly ministry]. Originally shame [words of community]; scared [threats by others]; quit church [could not stand criticism]; became incognito [avoided family resemblance]; special appearance [1-Cor. 15:7] saved [brethren of Lord]; knew of entrepreneurship [knew fathers business]; used by Christ [writer to Christian church]; acquainted w/economics; represents Jesus [treasures laid up]

At the time of this letter from James [AD-45], the church is under attack and seeking independence and self-sustaining capabilities seem out-of-reach. Men tend to tear one another down as a way of rising self above others [today]. So James leaves from the porch of slander and steps of detraction into the residence of pride [detraction is often couched in truth and clothed in fair language]. A poison infused with sugar and served in a golden cup [looking for blemishes, defects, to prevent or misrepresent things].

After Jesus' death and ascension, James comes back to Jerusalem and serves as one of the early elders of the church. In so doing, he thrusts himself into the Lord's life and work. Like us, he knows did not do right by his brother. And so he sets out to make up for lost time [anybody]. It seems that he has been around the merchants; listening to their conversations. As Jews moved about, they took their merchandise and sensed that they would always make a living if they worked hard enough. [good education, good job, good house, good life. He recognizes their plans [promote plans] but they did just what most of us do [left God out of the picture].

So James offered to settle one of their problems. They were looking for hope. Hope was what they needed. Disgusted; disgruntled, disappointed; diseased; devastated [hope].

He Cautions their Independence: America withheld certain freedoms from Negroes for a long time. We felt those freedoms were guaranteed by the US Constitution [life, liberty, and the pursuit of happiness]. History shows us a new kind of shackle [debt; envy; self-hate; worry; ulcers; early death]. Jews felt they were born free [under God] and so they wanted the freedom of speech. But James cautions (1) *watch what you say* [today or tomorrow we will]. We ought to watch what we say too [promises; vows w/o honor; help church but words hinder]. He cautions (2) *watch where you go* [we will go into such/such a city]. Some places we go are not good for us; some things we take up will hurt us in the long run; good now/bad later. Christian conduct is not sleazy; slowful; selfish; nasty; negative]. He cautions (3) *watch your stay* [sometimes we stay too long; friendships; where we work; neighborhoods]. He cautions (4) *watch what you do to make money and how you feel about it* [gain was taken by Ahab; for the love of $ is the root of all evil]. Beware of your desire for independence [Israel wanted to be free but made great gains while in slavery].

He Sees their Vain Confidence: James discovered something about himself when he looked back on his life. He feared the folk and felt shame for his brother. But it was his brother that could do what the folk could not do [heal; feed; comfort; bind; satisfy]. They planned their futures but James knew (1) *They had false confidence because of their inability to know the future* [you know what shall be tomorrow]. Life is like that [Alexander; Saul; Lincoln]. (2) *James warned them about confidence in life for it is uncertain* [what is your life?] Vapor; [like a morning mist; spreads; frail and ever changing; iced tea] Job described it as few days/ full of trouble; time is a thief; life is filled w/swift transition]. Great civilizations are built upon the principle of far-seeing prudence. Yet there can be a false use of this true principle. Many have an unchristian reliance on the future and have become engrossed in plans for its direction. Life is not like a bowl of cherries. (3) *James warned them against false confidence in lasting life* [it appears for a little while]. This is a foolish and irrational spirit to expect a successful future w/o God @ the center. It is wicked for a finite and sinful man to cherish the proud confidence that he may map out the future of his life at his own pleasure. To act as if the keys of time were in one's own hand. Or that the assurance of life and health are papers locked up in a fire resistant safe. This involves an arrogance that in essence is really sin. This thinking originates in pride [the fountain of all sin]. Our evil spirit makes an idol of self. [I am not going to put up with that; not me; willi-fu/fu]. Do not thrust God out of His own world.

He Assures Us of Dependence: James lets his mind stroll back down memory lane. He senses his own false love of the world. He got out of town to avoid being known as the brother of Jesus. That is the sign of loving this life. (1) *He encouraged them to realize their dependence on God.* [V-15 "for you ought to say, if the Lord will"] This presents a true view of life. His governance of human existence. [fate; chance; destiny] all governed by His will. We trust men and things that have been around for a short time rather than He that has been around forever. [famous; elected; houses; cars; army; bullets and bombs; missiles; television; new medicines] We have little faith in God and His ability to address our every need. [mercy; grace; love; truth; started - will complete] (2) *James sets hope on its' end when he reminds them of failure to depend on God*. They had talked of "trade, and get gain" in vs.-13. But in vs-16 he recalls the parable his brother offered about the rich fool that received an abundant harvest, but tried to lay up treasures for many years. James knew that the gains on men's hearts extend beyond material ones [position; power; fame; intellectual achievements] It matters not what they are, if they be sought covetously and selfishly, they fall under a false love of the world. Rejoicing in boasting [bragging; what I got/done/have]. He closes this part of the epistle with (3) _a warning about the resistance of dependence on God_. Our love for the earth has caused us to avoid doing what we know is right. There is a relationship between knowledge and responsibility. [to whom much is given, much is required] Many of them were failing to practice what they clearly understood to do. [moving from city to city they did not feel compelled to pay tithes and offerings] Not my pastor; not my church; they have not done anything for me. Sometimes we know to do good, but will not do it. [dislike of the person; thing; memory] James says here that our guilt will be greater. The church was established on the blood of Christ. Set there for all men and for all times. [evil; thieves; murderers; adulterers; liars] But the church is set there for those that feel morally pure but have never sought the forgiveness and grace of God. [haters; deceivers; filled with envy; jealous; wishers] We are the threads of life that make love real in this world. Life is filled with swift transition. None on earth can really stand. Build your hope on things eternal. Hold to God's unchanging hand.

Closing: James does not leave us w/o solid proof of denying the sadness of our trust in temporary things. He leads into chapter-V with explicit evidence about holding out hope for things. When we trust in the treasures of this life, we will ultimately become _selfish_. Then we will move to _injustice_ Lastly, it will move to _murder._ Remind them of America's period of slavery.

Remind them of the feast @ Belshazzar's ball.

Tell the Story of the pilot named James Stockdale [1965 shot down in Vietnam] End with <u>this may be the day</u>!

Sermon – Legion
Mark Chapter-5 vss. 2-20

Introduction: By giving us the extreme case of Legion, Mark assures us that we all fall within the boundaries of the caring power of Christ. [given to you to know the mysteries of the Kingdom]. If you know characters in the Bible you know He cares for us all. It does not make Him a difference [he cares for us all]. It does not matter if you are old/ugly; rich/poor; up/down; witch/wonderful; popular/hated; industrious/lazy; he cares. To prove my case, He cared for a widow @ Nain, mother-in-law, woman with the issue of blood, Bartimaeus, man let down through the hole in the roof, Mary-Magdalene the prostitute, adulterer, Simon the leper, man @ Solomon's porch for 38 years.

Christ had just tamed a wild sea. Now He comes to tame a wild man. Warning [wild men]. This is not just a tall tale. [Truth]. Legion is the picture of Satan's finished product [made, miserable, masquerade, mighty, misunderstood, mastered]. Legion is the destroyed image of God in man. [spiritless, powerless, friendless, homeless, penniless, loveless]. But the power of Christ is victorious in the case of Legion. Legion could be one of us. Legion could be most of us. Legion could be all of us.

A Man Under Bondage to Evil: There are _dangerous effects_ of sin. Legion faced Jesus as a rejected man. [unclean] He was probably rejected from childhood. He was probably rejected by the whole community. He was rejected by his past [it haunted him] and by the diagnosis of those around him. Finally he rejected himself in despair. The door by which the devil entered his life was the door called rejection. [warning]. By the indulgence of appetite and habit people are conquered. Legion had no self-control. This is the mark of those possessed. Look at the drunkard and his downward spiral. Look at the gambler and his losing ways. Look at the drug addict and his belief that he can overcome. Look at the spender and her thoughts that she can "quit when she gets ready".

There are _deranging effects_ of sin. He selected an unusual place to stay. He was dwelling in a place most folk fear [tombs]. The prodigal must come to himself before he can return to his father. He had lost all feelings [cut himself with stones]. The Bible says.."for this cause, God gave them over". He had suffered amiss of moral sensibilities. He caused others terror and misery. Stopped folk from having burials. Stopped folk from coming to out flowers on their loved one graves. Grounds crews could not even mw the graveyard.

A Man Casting Off Human Restraints: Legion was the object of negative solutions. [possessed] His keepers [they loved him] could do nothing but confine and restrict him. There had been little improvement using that approach. [they would not change]. For life's worst cases we still offer only negative and confining solutions. Domestic comfort is gone. Respect for others and by others was lost. Life was laid waste. He could see fingers pointed @ him. He could see eyes glaring @ him. He heard the insults leveled against him. He watched as others avoided him. Human restraint will never conquer moral evil. It represses it or alters it but never roots it out. [prejudices; blue laws; dry counties; abortions; teen pregnancies; church house and church folk]. The disorder and restlessness seen in society highlight serious problems and indicate a breakdown of values in our civilized world. [enron; arthur anderson; WWF; athletes and drugs; oil and pollution; loving God and hating your brother]. We may restrain dishonesty [children see it], drunkenness [children], swearing [children], cheating [children] so that it is not seen in public, but the hypocrisy is visible to an "all-seeing" eye. The demonic slipped his chains and is there in the open. Legion faces Jesus as a divided man. [hypocrite] Part of him wants to fall down before Christ and worship vs-6. Another part wants to stand up to Jesus and question Him vs-7. Another part of him demands that Jesus not bother him vs-7(d). Still, another part of Legion desires to run away from Christ. Legion both hated and loved himself as he was. That is the problem of all of us. He met a Judge he could not deceive. He dreaded being near a King he could not escape. So do we!

A Man Meeting His Saviour: With his morbidly quickening senses, he admits he knows who Jesus was and he knew what was coming. He takes a daring misuse of the sacred name and indicates the distractions and disorder that make him who he is. Jesus faces Legion wisely, firmly, and lovingly. _Wisely_, as an accepting person. This is noted in the simple asking for a name. Jesus asked Legion for his name so that Legion could own who he was. You cannot disown what you have become until you own what you have become. [sobriety; debt-free; sinners/saved]. Legion had to admit that he was full of division, which his name suggests. [no man can serve 2 masters]. Jesus gave Legion a positive solution. Calmly, Jesus says "come out of him". You will note the illustrated aspects of evil. It frightened the swine. Evil drives animals crazy.

Jesus dealt with Legion _firmly_. Jesus waited and gave Legion time to think about what need he had for help. [we never give people time]. Christ wait with hope over the possibilities [with Christ, all things are possible]. Legion saw the hogs run into the sea. He needed to see that; so that he would know that God's forgiveness is bigger than man' sin. Often we make sin and guilt bigger than God's grace.

Jesus dealt with Legion _lovingly_. Because of the power of Christ, a divided man became whole. And in a short time, he was to be seen sitting at the feet of Jesus, clothed, and in his right mind. Christ does not come to make us a "little better". He comes with awesome power to restore life to its fullness. [I've come, that they might have life and life abundantly]. That part that wanted to come to Jesus ultimately overcame that part that wanted to run away from Jesus.

Closing: In each of us, the dominion of sin must be broken. Only Christ can break it. It was when his friends had given up on this man as hopeless [demoniac] that his redemption came. Jesus' death, burial, and resurrection. When self-reform has proven useless. When benefactors fail. When friends and loved ones lose heart. He proves "able to save to the uttermost". Dealing pitifully with the sinner, He deals ruthlessly with our sin [casts them into the sea of forgetfulness].

Story of believers down @ riverside for baptism

Sermon – News for America
Matthew Chapter-IX vss. 35-38

Introduction: If you look around in America today, you would see great concerns and issues that cloud and color life in a dark gray. Blackouts are but a symptom of spiritual depravity [no lights; no electricity; no enthusiasm or spirit]. Terrorism is but a taste of the misery our country began with KKK [avoid the truth, drive fear in men; hide your faces while doing it]. Joblessness is but a sample of the lack of seriousness man has exhibited towards God [not willing; stingy; self-centered].

But our text points out the same conditions for Palestine during our Lord's earthly ministry. America has promoted homelessness [same then]. America has passed laws that no longer shelter the sick and infirmed [blind begging, lepers loose; no aid for ADA]. America has passed laws that deny medical benefits to the poor [woman w/issue of blood]. America has lowered the poverty standards and refuses help for the lower classed citizens [widow's mite; need to feed 5000; cheating the poor @ Temple]. America has put justice up for sale [questioned Jesus about His authority].

But I believe Jesus is passing through America just like Matthew describes His walking in that day. He sees our nation, as we are now; harassed like a hunted animal with bin Laden holding the gun. We appear helpless with exhaustion and broke from defense, yet needing more money to keep up the fight Iraq; Liberia; Cuba; rebels, villains, Monrovia, etc]. I believe He sees the potential for abundant spiritual response; yet He assesses the small number of willing workers. He feels for America. A land of the free. Home of the brave. A land that prints, "in God we trust" on its money yet will not trust God with its' money. His compassion moves Him inwardly to the core. He even offers a solution. Out of our deepest desires, we are to plead with God the Proprietor of the harvest to thrust workers into the fields of America. For indeed the harvest is ripe; but the laborers are few.

The Lord Passes Through America: The good news is that *Jesus had a habit* and always wants to go through any land. In Matt. 4:23, Jesus went about all Galilee teaching and preaching the gospel of the Kingdom as well as healing all manners of sickness. When Lazarus was dead, he wanted to go back through Samaria [Thomas thought they would die; met woman @ well, whole town saved]. That was his habit back then and I believe it is His desire today.

As He moved through those towns, *His habit was to preach the good news*. He did so not for gain, not for pleasure, but for love. He saw people neglected and without care. He got angry looks. He saw men speaking under their breaths. He understood that anger inside was a malicious decay that destroys those that hate.

He also had a _habit of caring for the sick_. The passage says he healed every sickness and every disease. Not like doctors today that refer you when they have done all they can do. We must be like Jesus. Waiting on all those that we know need our help. [liars; gamblers; double-tongued; backbiters; cursers; cheaters; thieves; streetwalkers; hungry; fatherless].

For the souls of men far outweigh their physical showings. The bad news is that America knows of 22,000 sites for churches and will not help them build.

The Lord Feels for America: The good news is that the Lord Jesus sees our nation as we really are. He feels our national pain. As Jesus moved hither and thither, He saw the great crowds and felt _compassion_. He was the Good Shepherd and concerned about His sheep. He knew and now knows where the green pastures were. He knew then and now knows where the still waters were. The flock was scattered [America is divided and not together] some of us are cast down [haves and have-nots] some wandering [alone and seeking friends] bruised [child abuse and spousal abuse is rampart] and their fleeces torn by wolves [having committed sins they cannot get forgiveness even from those that have been forgiven]. The Pharisees despised the poor and those that had met misfortune. They began to hate Jesus because He cared for the poor. [what about us?] "Jesus came to seek and to save the lost".

But we are part of His _observation:_ He saw them, wounded, hurting, in doubt, weary, affected with spiritual evils and physical illness. We are exhausted. Tired of struggling and ready to drop in our tracks. Our best is not good enough. Our efforts are met with scorn. We get the worst for our best; bad/good; frown/smiles; deceived by loved ones; last hired and first fired. In America today, the popular message is wealth [churches growing]. But leave sin alone [let us do what we want to do].

The Lord Prays for America: The good news for us is that the Lord _recognizes the potential_. In vs. 37 He says to His disciples "the harvest is truly plentiful". We see here the figure begins to change. The people were His flock but now we hear them called His harvest [gains; huge gatherings]. The world is overflowing with needs for God's love [Israel/Egypt]. The underlying truth is that hate is ripening, people are tiring, the gap between those with and those without is widening.

The Lord also _recognizes the problem_. In verse 37 He says.."but the laborers are few". Woman that aborted babies need counseling [none available]. Those that tried to wreck homes need somebody to lift them [all alone]. Criminals that got caught need a loving hand to help [everybody turned their backs]. We have made it impossible to repent in public. Sneers and jeers, laughter and smirks await those that testify of failure. Folk do not want anybody to know about mistakes. Jesus knows all about our problems, He will guide until the day is done; there is not a friend like the lowly Jesus, no not one, no not one.

The Lord _recommends the plan._ [pray] Jesus exhorts the disciples to pray to fix the problem. The soul of a man is more important than his body. Yet we pray that the body will be healed rather than the soul. God cares deeply for this harvest. He cares so deeply that He sent His only begotten Son to die for that harvest. Oh, that prayer would be offered up for the assistance of Almighty God to send His Holy Spirit to aid our efforts. James said..The effectual, fervent prayer of the righteous availed much [success depends on prayer]. Nothing is beyond the reach of prayer. Jesus Himself said all things, whatsoever you ask, in prayer, believing, you shall receive.

<u>Closing:</u> It is in the strength of the prayer of the church that preachers pursue their solemn work. When they fail, when they stumble in faith, leave from humility, stop their visits in love, depart from this self-denying labor, the fault may lie in part with those that forget to pray according to the Lord's commandment.

Pray without ceasing!

Story of missionary that went because His church agreed to pray.

Sermon ~ A Day to Leave Difficulties Behind

("Stand still, and see the deliverance of the Lord")
Exodus   Chapter-XIV   Verses 10-14

Introduction:
The scene of the text is on the banks of the Red Sea. [similarities to man]
Fear grips the present and makes one lose sight of the future. [Egypt Vs. Canaan]
430 years of slavery [type of sin] has been met by prayer and answered by proclamations.

- The Problems with Pharaoh [Pharaoh insults God]
- The Promise by the Almighty [God assures Moses that He will deliver the Jews]
- The Prophet appointed [Aaron becomes a spokesman for Moses]
- The Power of God mentioned [God mentions to Moses divine wrath]
- The Preliminaries [confronted by Moses/Aaron, he demands a demonstration]
- The Plagues [blood-frogs-gnats-flies-murrain-boils-hail-locusts-darkness-death]
- The Preparation [God gives them instruction about the Passover]
- The Protection [God will kill all firstborn, but reassures that "when I see blood"]
- The Panic [Pharaoh summons Moses, and demands they leave Egypt]
- The Presents [terrified Egyptians give parting gifts to the Israelites]

One suggests that with this much evidence, people can trust God. 430 yrs vs. 1-day

Tonight, we have come to wait for the recorded second of man's timepiece [Midnight]
But, every day we live, we constantly seek that day when we can leave difficulties behind
While these words are the words of the natural Redeemer, Moses, they represent God.

These words contain the great command to the believer [believer] when in trouble.

This voice is a confidence to those saints that are brought to extraordinary difficulties.

Debt [spiraling out-of-control] _Sickness_ [sapping away the strong virtues of life] _Aging_.

Alone [in doubt that you are needed/wanted] _Afraid_ [not knowing which way to turn]

The believer cannot retreat, he cannot go forward. Shut up on the right/left hand. ???

What must we do in this coming year.........."Stand Still"

It will be well for those that heed this command.

Listen only to the voice of the Master, although other advisers make their suggestions.

Despair, Cowardice, Impatience, Presumption will recommend but Faith says [stand still]

Inspection:

Despair whispers _"they come after us" [v-10]_ lie down and die, give up, [they know]

Some of us are always looking behind us. Paul says forget behind, press forward

Last year may have been a year of defeats [despair reminds] Sampson

God wants cheerful courage. At the worst of times-rejoice in love and faithfulness

Cowardice whispers _"why did you bring us out of Egypt to die" [v-11]_ Go back to sin.

Retreat to the world's way of doing it. You cannot be a Christian! No good.

Relinquish your principles. That church is not growing. They will never get there.

If you are a child of God [or ever hope to be] stand still even when weak.

Knowing that "we can do all things through Christ who strengthens us".

What if called to stand still for a time? Renew thy strength for advancing.

Everything in life is to renew. [trees-plants-weather-skin-clothes-faith]

Impatience whispers, "_leave us alone to continue the present" [v-12a]_

Where you are is not the best place to be. But where you go is unknown to you.

Most would cry."do something, don't just stand there!"

But too often we have made the mistake of thinking that we could fix it ourselves.

Instead, we should look to the Lord. He will not only do something but everything

Presumption whispers, "_we were better off serving the Egyptians" [v-12b]_

We are not better off serving Satan. Sin causes destruction-damage-decline.

If we keep with our hate, we become slaves to hatred.

If we keep with our refusals to work together, we falsely represent a church.
If we cannot make progress, even after renewing our commitments, we fall behind
If we remain in Egypt, we can never enjoy Canaan.

- Hell-raisers get no Heaven.
- Stingy givers get no gold themselves
- Reason seekers never find righteousness
- Those that seek control of the Church will soon be "out-of-control"
- Followers of God soon discover that rainbow of promised peace

Although those voices seem right when trouble comes [New Year], Faith is lasting.

Introspection:
Faith whispers "*fear not, stand still", but only after listening to God. [v-13]*
-Faith says.."be ye steadfast, unmovable, always abounding in the word".
-Faith would say to you…"weeping may endure for a night, but joy cometh"
-Faith would tell you this new year that.."be of good courage, I have overcome"
-Faith would remind us that segregation fell to integration [after a struggle]
-Faith would remind us that the Iron Curtain @ Russia fell to Democracy.
-Faith would remind us that sin gives way to salvation. Fear to freedom
-Faith would remind us that crucifixion gives way to resurrection.
Stand [keep the posture of an upright man] do not bow or bend of yield
Stand still [do not interfere with His works] expecting further orders
See [remain on guard with watchfulness and soberness] ready for action
God will show you this day [days & days] It has been a long time, but not much longer

Pharaoh decided to follow-up [after he allowed the Israelites their freedom]
The people decided to give up [once they saw the Egyptian army chasing them]
Moses declared to the people to look up [depend on God to rescue you].
God decreed to Moses to lift up [Moses is told to raise his staff and divide the Sea]

Story of the Day Satan held a strategy session for subverting **salvation**!

- The 1st demon said, "there is no life after death" [man is not stupid]
- The 2nd demon said, "there is no God" [man believes] even if not following
- The 3rd demon said, "tell them God is real, the Bible is the true word of God".
- A 4th demon said, "yes, that will work, tell them Jesus died and they need not worry"

- A 5th demon agreed. Then we can help them make excuses for delaying their decision
- All the demons and the Devil began shouting for joy. This plan would work!!

Sermon ~ The Invitation
on the Last Day
John   Chapter-VII   verses 37-41

Introduction:

One of the rituals held during the Feast of Tabernacles [also called the Festival of Shelters] was the pouring out of large amounts of water in the Temple. This scene was a reminder to Israel that God had given the Jews water while they walked in the wilderness. Water for drinking pictures the Holy Spirit, who is given to those that trust in Christ. This whole world is thirsty. But we can only have this thirst quenched by coming to Jesus Christ.

There had been *ridicule* from His half-brothers and sisters.

There had been a *recommendation* to move His miracles to another location.

Jesus had *responded* that the world hated Him because He exposed their sins.

There had even been a challenging *reaction* to the Lord.

- Some felt He was a good man. [11-12]
- Some felt He was a deceiver. [13]
- Some felt He was demon-possessed. [20]
- Some felt He was just an ordinary man. [25-27]
- Some felt He was a Prophet. [40]
- Some felt He was the Messiah. [31, 41]

The people wanted to arrest Him. But could not because of the Pharisees.

The Pharisees wanted to arrest Him but could not. [The soldiers]

The Military wanted to arrest Him but could not. [No man ever spoke like that man]

The parliament wanted to arrest Him but could not. [Nicodemus]

God always protects those that do His will. In this terrible scene, Jesus issues His invite.

Inspection:

Patience had her perfect work in the Lord Jesus, and even until the last day of the feast, He pleaded with the Jews. Yes, eve on the last day of the year, He will plead with us, and waits to be gracious to us. This is admirable indeed. The long-suffering Savior bears with some of us year after year, notwithstanding our provocations, rebellions, and resistance of His Holy Spirit. Wonders of wonders that we are still in the land of mercy.

Pity expressed herself most plainly, for Jesus cried out, which implies not only the loudness of His voice, but also the tenderness of His tones. He entreats us to be reconciled. "We pray you", says the Apostle, as though God did beseech you by us. How deep must be the love of the Lord that makes Him weep over sinners. And what compassion He must have to serve as does a mother that woos her children to the bosom for their own protection. You would believe that we would all come

at such a cry. That even unwilling hearts would be willing to come.
Provision is made most plenteous; all is provided that can need to quench his soul's thirst.

To his conscience, the atonement will bring peace.

To man's understanding, the gospel will bring the richest instruction.

To man's troubled heart, the person of Jesus is the noblest object of affection.

To the starving mind of man, Christ will bring the purest nutriments.

To the sickest body of man, Jesus brings speedy healing that amazes the masses.
Thirst is terrible. [No death is heard to be more dreadful]
Although the soul is famished because of sins, Jesus can restore it to life.
Proclamation is made most freely, that every thirsty one is welcomed. No other distinction is required. [Thirsty] Whether it is a hint of avarice, ambition, pleasure, knowledge, rest, employment, promotion, or security, he or she that suffers from any of these is invited to come. The thirst itself may be bad in itself, and there may not be a sign of deliverance, but a sin that longs to be gratified by even more swallows of the sad water of sin. But it is not the goodness of the man that invites. It is the goodness of God, the grace and mercy of His love that calls us to come. The Lords sends it freely, and without respect of persons.
Personality is declared most fully. The sinner must come to Jesus, not to works, rituals, ordinances, or doctrines, but to a personal Redeemer, who bare our sins in His own body on the Cross. The mistreated, beaten, bleeding, dying, rising Savior, is the only star of hope to a sinner. Oh for the right to come now and drink. No waiting line. No "take a number". No price list. Just come.

Introspection:
Drinking here represents a reception for which no fitness is required.

- Fools [full of folly]
- Ignorant [refusing to accept instruction]
- Thieves [those that steal time and attention]
- Losers [those that participate in the invisible game of mastery]
- Harlots, gamblers, destroyers, etc.

Sinfulness of character is no barrier to those that can come and drink.
Jesus does not mean the need of a golden cup. He does not require a jeweled chalice. No bucket or glass in which to convey the water of the thirsty.

- The mouth of poverty can come.
- The mouth of stupidity can stoop and drink.
- The blistered lips of stolen kisses can also come and drink.
- Filthy hands can hold this unseen cup of love and care.

Jesus is the fountain of hope for all of us. He is the one that calls us to come.

Close with the story of the man who was thirsty but would not drink behind another because of the threat of polluting the water. But with Jesus, we cannot pollute the source of this water.

Sermon ~ Confidence in a Savior
Luke   Chapter-I   verses 26-34

<u>Introduction:</u>

This Sunday is the one Sunday of this year when Christians celebrate a new beginning.

It should be a day filled with excitement and joy [contrary-it becomes a day of fear] confident!

Isaiah the Prophet [9:2] looked toward this day and called it *Incomparable*.

He knew that people had walked in darkness but now sat in darkness.

This baby [Jesus] born so ordinary, would do extra-ordinary things.

His birth [super natural] we celebrate, explains our new birth [supernatural].

The passage explains that this event [Christ's birth] followed 400 yrs. of darkness.

Every OT passage historically outlined a Redeemer after periods of darkness.

So this day comes @ a time when the world thought God had forgotten them.

Words [prophets-priests-kings-patriarchs-called] seemed empty. Preacher's words!

Trouble makes us fear. Pain-pretense-darkness-loneliness-uncertainty-faithlessness.

But God comes to the virgin Mary w/ the words "Fear Not" during her crisis.

Although the birth of Christ is not a crisis, somebody today needs to hear "fear not".

<u>Inspection:</u>

<u>There is the fear of the unexpected ["fear not, Mary"]</u>

    Stable [Mary's life up until then had been very normal]

    Surprise [this news brought waves to her peaceful harbor]

      a. The angel brought an easy panic to the unexpected.

      b. She had plans to get married. This ruined her plans.

      c. Some fear all interruptions. Competition. Calls. Letters. Summons.

    Subdued [The angel brought good news, Mary had found favor with God]

<u>Then, there is the fear of personal loss [Joseph</u>
<u>wondered what the people would say]</u>

    Reputation [Mary was a special girl in the city. No reputation for bad behavior].

    Remarks [A girl pregnant before marriage created a scandal]. Gossip! Selfish!

    a. Joseph's dreams were shattered. His castles came tumbling down

    b. He thought he would lose all he hoped for. [trusting in man's opinion]

    c. How real are our fears about our children, husbands/wives, parents, jobs]

Please note that Joseph was not afraid of the angel, but of the loss.
>   *Resistance* [we fear losing, money-home-good name-jobs-cars-reputations]
>   *Refrain* [we hold back and God holds our blessings] afraid to love-invest-live]
>   *Results* [Joseph would not lose Mary, but would gain more than imagined].

Finally, there is the fear of meeting God [Zacharias,
the priest feared when he saw Him]
>   Reverent fear *[the shepherds feared because of His glory]*
>   Respectful fear *[Many others have feared Christ] Abraham-Job-Peter-Isaiah*
>   *Resentful fear* [Herod-Pilate-Jewish leaders]
>   *Remindful fears* [many today fear meeting God] sins-failures-poor attitudes.
>   *Reduced fears* [God loves us and sent His Son to be our Savior]

Introspection:
Fear comes when no human eye penetrates the darkness of sin. But be confident!!

Adam and Eve sinned and the prince of darkness ruled.

But Jesus, the light of the world, came as a baby [manger-wrapped] to reign.

The prince of death was in control. But the Lord of life came as an infant to overtake.

The power of mortality thrust every generation into the graveyard without hope.

But the Baby born in Bethlehem will banish all of the enemy's powers of immortality.

God's love seems even greater when we realize what He left to come here.

No doubt, if He had not been God Himself, He may have had fear of the world.

Remember Peter on the sea when the storm came. How he got over it when Jesus came.

Story of witnessing the gospel and how God gave us something to say. [fire]

Sermon-God Crowns A King

Psalms   Chapter-II   verses 1-12

Even though we live in a democracy, God intends to rule His people with a monarch.
While we in America expect a president, God wants us to enjoy a King.
In the Old Testament, God expressed the identification of David and his heirs [rule Israel]
God even pointed to Jerusalem as the location for this dynasty to reign.
But because of the failure of His people and the world's rejection this never happened.

But regardless of popular belief, God's promise did not fail.
In the city of Bethlehem, the city of David, a family member came to take the throne
Humankind begged for a greater than David or Solomon, and He came [Jesus Christ]
Today, only those that are true members of His body the Church recognize Him
Ultimately, every knee and nation will bow to His rule.

This psalm was written for the coronation of an OT king.
But its greater fulfillment is the coronation of the King of Kings.
God crowns Christ King and gives Him all nations as His coronation present
Although the nations of the world rebel against God's choice, it is a foolish thing
Why…because God crowns a King

___

The Apostates Reject

What is the most appropriate diagnosis of the human condition? Is it poverty, the lack of learning, or even psychological sickness? The most accurate description of the human condition is rebellion against God.

Here, the psalmist looks with amazement as creation rebels against its Creator. "Why do the nations conspire and the peoples plot in vain?" v1 God is astonished and even indignant that the nations and sovereigns of the earth refuse to submit to Him. The language depicted here indicates a kind of slogan or community opposite of reality. [United Nations Against God]. It is an imaginary picture of a great crowd's uproar. It is a photograph of huge convention where people hatch a plot and develop platforms that demand a vote against God.

If you review history, you will find a vivid demonstration of this rebellion. The OT never recognized Israel's king as the anointed ruler. At the birth of Christ, neither did Rome nor Jewish elders accept Jesus as King. Caesar Augustus. Herod the Great. Caesar Tiberius. Pilate failed to recognize Jesus as King. The sum and substance of history is plain revolt against God. But before we sniggle and grin [we too don't recognize Jesus]

Today, that is still true. The rule and reign of God is not taken into serious consideration. Man is yet in revolt. V-3 tells that we still want to break the chains and throw off the fetters of God's rule for our lives. But what is true of the nations is also true of individuals. Ask yourselves if you willingly submit to the rule and reign of God in your life.

The Almighty Responds

Although we reject God, human rejection does not threaten God. On the earth, rejection towards one another stings [love, jobs, singing, talking, listening, divorce, rejections]

But in verse-4 we see God laughs at us when we reject Him. It lets us know that God's reaction to the rage of the nations against His rule is closer to the human laugh than anything else. God's response if different than ours.

God also can quickly dispatch human rejection. When rejection persists, God speaks and His word is power. His indignation will vex, confound, trouble, and strike with terror the mere men that oppose His will. If you doubt this, just look at the end of time and how He will deal with those that stand in opposition to Him.

God's only answer is His only Son. In verse-6 you would expect a great battle against the rebellious earth. But instead you read the edict in the words.."I have installed my King on Zion, my holy hill". God's reaction was not a great battle. He answers with the promise of a baby, a little infant, the greater son of David. At a time when one would expect a clash of weapons or a thunderbolt from Heaven that vaporizes a rebellious planet, God sends a baby to Bethlehem.

God's answer for your personal rebellion is His son. He wants to come to terms with you and me through Jesus Christ. He even tells us that we can accomplish our good success if we just "kiss the son" in verse-12.

The Anointed Reigns

Today, one question asked by many is what is the destiny of our planet. Will it really collide with a meteor, or bomb itself into oblivion? The intention of God is to give the earth to His Son. In verse-8 He says.."ask of me and I will make the nations your inheritance, the ends of the earth your possession". This was the promise of the father. These words came to fulfillment in Matt. 28:18 when our Lord rose from the earth and claimed…"All power in Heaven and Earth is in my hands". But these words will find their ultimate permanency when Christ reruns to the earth to rule forever.

The characteristic of the rule of Christ will depend on our response. For those that yield, He will "herd them like sheep with the crook of iron". Firm, stable, unbending lordship will mark His reign on earth. For those that refuse to yield, there will be easy, complete, uncorrectable destruction. They will be shattered into fragments, which cannot be put together again. [humpty-dumpty].

God intends to give the earth to His Son as a result of our witness to all nations. When that happens, the earth will come. God wants to take possession of you before He takes possession of the earth. God wants us to yield our lives to His rule before He ruins our lives. We should serve the Lord with reverent fear.

<u>Closing</u>

We refuse to line up with the Lord because we cannot accept criticism [dealing w/Samaritans].
Criticism [skunk-dead] [moon-barking] [ruined by praise rather than saved by criticism]
The Israelites missed the gifts of Canaan because of their rebellion against truth
We mortgage the joy of the future for a moment of pleasure in the present.
We rebel against God because we fear the people's talk [Peter's denial]
Rebellion is like the lady who refused to look in the mirror [never see ourselves]

Sermon-Christ Calls Us, Come and Rest

Matthew   Chapter-XI   Verses 28-30

<u>Introduction</u>
-If we were to look across the Earth today, we would see people everywhere in trouble.
-It seems that all that we do never brings us a moment's rest.
-We scramble, ramble, and even gamble to gain that time when all seems at ease.
-However, it just does not take place.
-Rest is important to man. After all God Himself took a rest.
-During the week of creation, God spent almost 15% of His time, resting.
-Man thought work would satisfy Him, but it never did.
-Man even thought vacation would satisfy him, but it never does.
-So today man seeks something that will do for him what rest did for God.
-We exhaust our patience and turn it into pity trying to get past pain for real rest.
-But it seems that no matter what we do, rest is elusive, intrusive, and exclusive.
-Jesus Christ is the inexhaustible Person.
-Only He stands before times and places with an offer to give everyone who comes, rest.
-This Earth can hardly sustain itself or those in need.
-When you consider us, we are so weary ourselves, we cannot help others.
-Unlike us, Jesus offers a river of rest that runs afresh from higher sources.
-His offer never stops, drops, hops, neither does it droop, stoop, loop.
-The record shows that the more rest He gives, the more He seems to have to give.
-Pastor Wm. Roberts of Princeton decided [no vacation] read [Gospels] Jesus rested.

> In summary, Jesus offers us the initial rest of salvation. We can never rest until we know for certain that guilt for us and alienation from God has been removed. But my friends, even beyond that, Jesus gives us the rest we find in discipleship. There is a deeper rest beyond that initial rest. That is the rest of wearing a toke that is styled by Christ. It is designed, crafted, and prepared by the Lord Himself.

-Believe me today, Jesus offers us initial rest and then continual rest.
-But all we have to do is come to Him.

- So if you are weary and heavy laden this afternoon, come.
- If you are troubled and in despair, come.
- If you are down and don't know where to turn, come.

Jesus calls! Come and Rest.

Jesus Offers Rest in Salvation

Every religious movement and each spiritual leader offers rest.
Even philosophical schools claim satisfaction from the tensions of life.
But towering over all, Jesus promises rest to the weary [the struggle for meaning to life].

- ### *Jesus offers His rest in a great invitation [Come to Me]*

His word is both a command that pushes us and an invitation that draws us.
Only Jesus has the royal authority to command us to approach Him.
Consider how stupid these words would be from someone else.
Life traps us in quicksand. We try to get out. But the more we twist, the more we risk.
Unless Christ crisply calls us up and out, we sink.
Our Lord's invitation is not to theology/personality; organization/organism;
institution/instinctive ness; celebration/celebrant; ritual/righteousness.
These 2 verses reverberate with the personal pronouns me, I, and my.
Rest comes only from the Person of Christ.

- ### *Jesus offers rest specifically for those invited [all those that are weary and laden]*

Those that are actively toiling and passively loaded down in life.
In our toil, we seek fulfillment in human work, activities, beliefs.
But work becomes labor. Activities become disillusionment. Beliefs become clowns.
Beyond our jobs, there is a lacerating pull to search life and find meaning.
In addition, we bear the loads of life, including expectations from others.
Many times, the commands others place upon us, they cannot perform themselves.
Jesus invites those in the rat race of religion to come and rest.
He becks for those bent over with dead weight of impossible expectations to come/rest.

- ### *Jesus offers spiritual rest because that is His intention [I will give you rest]*

Spiritual rest does not come from religion, rituals, routine, reflection, or redundancy.
Unlike the Pharisees, Sadducees, Herodians, and Romans, Christ could deliver rest.
Pharisees [education] Sadducees [money] Herodians [theory] Romans [politics]
Jesus offers and can give us the power to be and to do what He requires.
This rest is significant. Christ gives rest from guilt, disfavor with God, and the chain of lust.
His death on the cross is strong enough to release us from guilt.
His resurrection is strong enough to restore us from disfavor to fellowship with

God.

His living again refreshes from that bondage of desire, because He lives in us.

Jesus Offers Rest in Submission

Beyond the initial rest of salvation, there is a deeper rest in submission.

At the start of the Christian's life, we gain a new experience called recovery.

Under the continuing lordship of Christ, we enter into deep rest.

As we review the methodology of gaining deeper rest the paradox of a yoke comes up.

Usually, when things are heavier, they burden us down.

But with the yoke of Christ, we are not burdened but freed. Not troubled/ triumphant.

Not hurt/healed. Not pained/promoted. All we do is take His yoke upon us.

■ *There is the necessity of a yoke [take my yoke upon you]*

Absolute freedom is an absolute illusion. A mirage man sees and finds gone @ arrival.

To be "free" in such a way is to experience the bonds of self-absorption.

That [brothers and sisters] is a yoke that chafes and drags, sags, bags life.

All of us will wear a yoke. Our own, somebody else's, or that of the Lord.

■ *There is the possibility of a superior yoke[take my yoke... and learn of me].*

By Jesus' time, the word yoke was already a common term for discipline/instruction.

The yoke was a sort of collar that channeled the energy and mind of a beast.

So, to wear the yoke of Christ is to channel the mind in a way we learn of Him.

Learn of His Person. Learn [Gospels] from Him. Learn His experiences/circumstances.

Self-satisfaction is self-delusion and harnesses us with a yoke that exhausts us.

The yoke used by Jesus is the warn embrace of the Master's love.

It acts like a hang-glider and lifts us above the toil of life. [misery, tears]

■ *There is also the simplicity of Jesus' yoke [I am meek and lowly in heart].*

That simplicity is the manner and method of the Master. He is gentle and mild.

Jesus is not proud, impulsive, ambitious, or desiring dominion over man. [meek inherits]

■ *There is the certainty of Jesus' yoke [you shall find rest for your souls].*

2 Thess I:7 tells us " And to those troubled, rest w/us, when Jesus is revealed in Heaven.

■ *There is also a quality of Jesus' yoke [My yoke is easy & my burdens are light].*

Easy yokes and light burdens really give rest for a man's soul.

The OT cried.."Ask where the good way is and find rest for your weary souls" [Jer 6:16]

So too, this great invitation is extended before the cross. Here Jesus does not tell us how.

But it is Jesus that makes the promise to us.

And when we know the **Who**, we ought never worry about the <u>How</u>

Closing

We see in His woeful death the morning of rest.

We see as well in His wonderful resurrection the daybreak of rest.

And, we see in His splendid ascension the noon of rest.

We see in His special role of Advocate, the nighttime of rest.

These are all temporary. Just as @ creation God made each thing. [light] [sky] [ground]

[sun-moon-stars] [birds-animals] [man] And on the 7th day, He rested.

He perfects them in dispensations of time. [innocence] [conscience] [human government]

[promise] [law] [grace] and….

One day, He will come back again, to receive us and take us to a place of REST!!

All men in every period sought rest. We seek rest. All after us will seek rest.

But true rest is only found in Jesus. I am too selfish. I am too partial. I am too weak.

But I know that since all of my steps are ordered, all of my stops must be ordered too!

Story of the Apostle John on the Isle of Patmos [handling the dove he kept as a pet].

Story of the great pitcher under stress in the World Series [going home to help Father].